W9-DDW-639

THE FAMOUS COOKERY COOKBOOK

The famous

BY GLORIA AGRIN JOSEPHSON

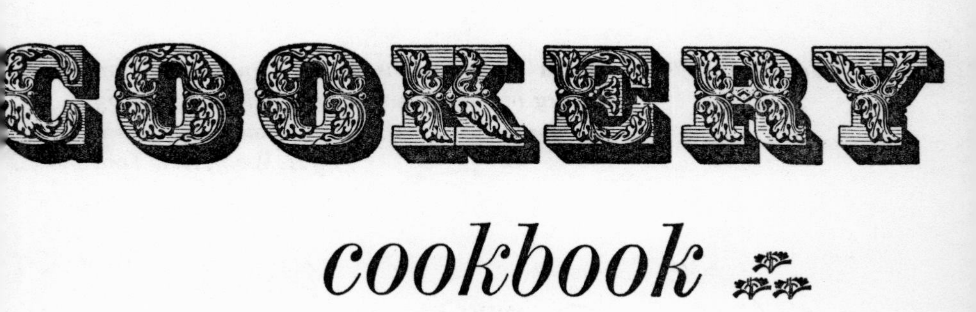

cookbook

ND BARNEY JOSEPHSON

with drawings by ANTON REFREGIER

HORIZON PRESS

New York

Library of Congress Catalog Number 63:13205
Manufactured in the United States of America
by H. Wolff, New York

A NOTE ABOUT

The famous COOKERY cookbook

This is a cookbook for everybody.

The recipes are designed for cooks—not chefs—to be prepared at home, where there are cooks, not chefs. The ingredients are the simplest—neither rare spices from the Orient nor truffles from Périgueux—nothing that cannot be found on a supermarket shelf. The dishes are chosen with respect for the budget-bound—no paté, no caviar—nothing that would extract your bottom budget dollar. Although in some respects, its culinary repertoire acknowledges the popular attachment to the ordinary, it entirely avoids the banal, but does not escape to the other extreme of the exotic—and often inedible. Not only does it contain directions for the perfected preparation of foods we know you already like, it also introduces many dishes we know you will grow to like. Great pleasures at the average family table is its express concern.

The experience of The Cookery—the restaurant for everybody—stands behind it.

THE AUTHORS

A NOTE ABOUT

The COOKERY

The Cookery is unique in many ways. In one particular way, it is especially unique: it is not just another restaurant. The Cookery Lafayette, the Cookery in the heart of New York's Greenwich Village, opened one Monday morning at 11 a.m.—November 17, 1955, to be exact. By Tuesday morning, it had become a Village institution, for those in the Village and for those who come to it. The Cookery, at 59th Street and Lexington Avenue—less ambitious in size and scope—which preceded it and has since been demolished, performed the same minor marvel. The Cookery Carnegie, at 56th Street and Avenue of the Americas—more ambitious in size and scope—which succeeded it, produced the identical phenomenon. Whatever its locale, The Cookery is a focal point of restaurant interest.

The Cookery, in a generic sense, is a success.

Its kind of success, however, is more than the success of a restaurant.

It is the success of a restaurant idea.

*There are, as every restaurant patron knows, expensive restaurants and inexpensive restaurants. The expensive ones are, by and large, good: good in decor, good in service, good in food. The inexpensive ones are largely bad in every way in which the others excel. That the desirable attributes of each—*i.e.* the pleasures of the one, the prices of the other—are necessarily mutually exclusive,* *is reflective of the prevailing mercantile hypothesis. The Cookery assumed to reconcile these opposites of the restaurant business on the theory that they were opposites by no inexorable law of either nature or restaurant economics.*

The Cookery's conception of restaurant operation is that its arithmetic is not so much a question of how much, but of what goes into what. Tasteful decor costs no more than cafeteria chrome, except for a turn of mind. Gracious service costs no more than hash-slinging, except for attention to an attitude. Ten dollar prime sirloins cannot be sold for $1.95, but good food can be served, nevertheless, with care for its selection, preparation and presentation. It can, moreover, be not merely good, but interesting and even exciting. The perspective of the Cookery was that an investment of costless intangibles, like blood, sweat, tears and imagination—added to money—could bridge the gap between quality and price.

This was the idea and it worked.

The Cookery, in operation, has absorbed the aesthetics of the fine restaurants. It has maintained—against the extraordinary odds of inflation—the prices of the modest ones. Its prices exclude no one at all able to afford restaurant food. Its quality, without regard to price, attracts all who choose restaurant dining. The Cookery is not just a restaurant; it is the restaurant for everybody.

CAVEATS!

In this cookbook:

tsp. *means* teaspoon
tbsp. *means* tablespoon
cup *means* 8 oz. measuring cup
oz. *means* ounce
lb. *means* pound
" *means* inch

Peel, cut, slice, crush, cook, boil, simmer, fry, brown, sauté etc. bear their common dictionary denotations.

All recipes are designed to serve 4, unless the recipe itself tells you otherwise.

VIVATS!

To my husband, without whose interlocutions this book would be a mere collection of recipes.

To my wife, without whose recipes this book would not be a cookbook.

contents

FROM THE GRILL, 25

FROM THE CASSEROLES, 75

i. chicken casseroles

ii. beef casseroles

ii. fried, indeed!

iii. poached, in a way!

iv. ah! omelets

v. pancaked eggs

vi. odd pans out

FROM THE SALAD BOARD, 141

i. fish

ii. fowl

iii. good red herring

iv. garnishes

v. dressings

SUPPER'S ON THE TABLE, *167*

i. french toast and french-toasted sandwiches

ii. made in france

iii. pancakes

iv. spécialités de la maison

from the grill

THE GRILL and the broiler rack are the primary instruments of cookery at the Cookery. Scratch the average American and, in his eating tastes, you will find a cave man. Give him meat! Neat! Meat, simple, unadorned, unameliorated, unelevated, unrelieved meat is the reflexive selection of the average Cookery customer. Whatever the range of the menu, the paramount demand is for steaks, chopped sirloins, beefburgers, ham steaks—br-r-r-oiled!—with potatoes!

Cookery variations on these very themes, however, have managed to insinuate themselves into the gastronomic repertoire of even the unreconstructed carnivores. These creations combine the known and desired with the more imaginative and less familiar to create dishes acceptable to the most primitive palate—and to the more sophisticated, a relief from alimentary *ennui.* In this quiet gustatory revolution, TERIYAKI has begun to take precedence over tenderloin and RUMAKI over plain F-R-I-E-D CHICKEN. Even casseroles are creeping into vogue.

If either your budget or your menu is in a rut, save the steak for Sunday and try some Cookery tricks with cuts and trimmings. You may even find, one day, the most retrograde meat-and-potatoes member of your family asking for HOCHEPOT DE POULARDE DU VIEUX-MOULIN. Then you will, indeed, have had it!

TERIYAKI

1½ lbs. broilable beef
1 green pepper, cut in ⅛s
4 pineapple chunks (fresh, frozen or canned)
4 small par-boiled (or canned) onions
½ cup cooking Sherry
½ cup soy sauce
½ cup water
1 clove garlic, mashed
¼ tsp. ginger (optional)

[*A note on the meat:* TERIYAKI can be made from good shell, porterhouse or sirloin steak, although that strikes us as an unnecessary extravagance. On the other hand, if it is prepared from inferior steak or some such as round or chuck, it will be inedible. The Cookery uses a cut called, in the trade, "hanger" or, in retail parlance, "butcher's tenderloin." It is inexpensive, has excellent flavor and is burdened by neither fat nor bones, once the thin outer sheath, like fell, is trimmed—by the butcher, if you can prevail upon him. It is as versatile a cut of meat as tenderloin and, in fact, derived its name from being the tenderloin favored by butchers—the one they traditionally take home. There is only one "butcher's tenderloin" to a steer, so that, in shops which do not normally stock them, it is wise to give your butcher fair warning of your intentions to deprive him of his take. The purchase of "butcher's tenderloin" may even become habit forming, for it can be used in so many ways (p. 26) other than for TERIYAKI.]

1. Cut the butcher's tenderloin lengthwise, along the center tendon, and remove it. This will leave two thick triangular strips of clean meat. Cut 10 chunks, about 2″ x 2″, from each strip.

2. Using 4 skewers, thread each one as follows: meat, green pepper, meat, onion, meat, pineapple, meat, green pepper, meat.

3. Mix the remaining ingredients to form a marinade.

4. Immerse the filled skewers in the marinade from 4 to 6 hours.

5. Remove the skewers of meat from the marinade and broil, over a grill or under a broiler, to the desired state of doneness, turning to brown on all sides. Broiling time depends on the size of the meat chunks and the heat of your oven or grill. Judge by checking one typical piece of meat where the skewer pierces it, the place likely to be least well done.

SERVE WITH: French fried potatoes, GRILLED POTATOES À LA MODE DE MA FEMME (p. 34), boiled rice or RICE PILAF (p. 30).

RUMAKI

1 2½ lb. frying chicken
1 ¾″ pre-cooked, boned ham steak
1 green pepper, cut in ⅛s
4 pineapple chunks (fresh, frozen or canned)
4 small par-boiled (or canned) onions
TERIYAKI marinade (p. 27)

1. Cut the chicken into pieces as follows: each leg, in half; each second joint, in half; each breast in half lengthwise and in half again crosswise; each wing, in half—in all, 20 pieces. If you are feeling prodigal, reserve the wings and legs for other purposes, and, instead, purchase another half chicken for the uses of this dish.

2. Cut the ham into 20 bits.

3. Using 4 skewers, thread each one as follows: chicken, ham, green pepper, chicken, ham, onion, chicken, ham, pineapple, chicken, ham, green pepper, ham, chicken.

4. Prepare the TERIYAKI marinade. Immerse the filled skewers in the marinade from 4 to 6 hours.

5. Remove the skewers from the marinade and broil, either over a grill or under a broiler, until well browned on all sides, at least 30 minutes.

SERVE WITH: Garniture suggested for TERIYAKI (p. 27).

SERVINGS: Serves 4 only if you are not hungry—2 or 3 otherwise, depending on the precise state of your appetite.

The "yakis," as we call them, are perfectly good as is. They are glistening and even more delicious when moistened—not drowned—in our tangy SOUTH SEA ISLAND SAUCE. *Any that is left—because the "clean" meat eaters may have demurred—is lush on baked ham and boiled tongue—where doctoring is* de rigueur*—or on roast chicken.*

SOUTH SEA ISLAND SAUCE

1 tbsp. oil
1 cup pineapple juice
1 tbsp. cornstarch
1 tbsp. soy sauce
3 tbsps. vinegar
6 tbsps. water
¼ cup ketchup
½ cup brown sugar
2 tbsps. pickling liquid from sweet mixed pickles (if possible)

1. Heat the oil and pineapple juice over a low flame until warm.

2. Mix the cornstarch, soy sauce, vinegar and water until smooth. Add this mixture to the juice-oil mixture.

3. Add the remaining ingredients and simmer until the sauce thickens, stirring constantly.

PRE-PREPARATION: This sauce may be made entirely in advance—even the day before—and re-heated before serving.

SERVINGS: That depends on how much sauce you like. It is certainly enough for one recipe of either TERIYAKI or RUMAKI.

RICE PILAF WITH RAISINS AND NUTS

4 tbsps. butter
1 cup rice, washed and dried
1 medium onion, chopped
½ cup almonds, chopped
½ cup white raisins
2 cups chicken stock or bouillon
2 cups water
2 tsps. salt

1. Melt the butter in a large skillet over medium heat. Add the rice and stir constantly until it is light brown, about 8 to 10 minutes.

2. Add the onions and continue to cook, stirring, for 5 minutes more.

3. Stir in the almonds, raisins, chicken stock, water and salt. Simmer slowly, uncovered, until the liquid has evaporated and the rice is soft, 30 to 40 minutes.

PRE-PREPARATION: The pilaf may be made in advance. One half hour before serving time, separate the rice into kernels with a fork. Add 2 tbsps. water, cover tightly and heat slowly.

A steak is a steak is a steak—with apologies to G. Stein—and a good steak is a good steak is a good steak. That is the whole trick in steak cookery; the rest is details. Prime shell, porterhouse or sirloin, cut thick—but not too thick—are good for broiling. Rather than broil bad steak, learn how to treat with less choice grades or to use, sometimes even more delectable, substitute cuts. With a touch of our imagination and a very little of your own effort, you need not dread any week that steak and the budget cannot co-exist.

BROILED STEAK

steak
stove, hot—very
butter (optional)

1. Trim every scrap of fat from the meat. If it is good meat, it will not become dry and you will avoid coating your steak with seared grease. Score the remaining rim of fiber to prevent curling.

2. Pre-heat your oven at a broil flame for at least 15 minutes. It should be *hot*.

3. Broil the steak until it is done to your taste. Top it with a lump of butter. SHALLOT BUTTER (p. 33), if your side dishes are simple enough, is an even more flavorful touch.

The time it takes for a steak to reach the desired state of doneness depends on your own oven; heat varies. A quick guide would be:

1″ steak:	8 min. (rare);	10 min. (med.)
1½″ steak:	12 min. (rare);	15 min. (med.)

Any steak under 1 inch should be sautéed (p. 36), not broiled; any over 1½ inches should be made into two steaks, for to broil it so that it is properly cooked within, will make it dry and tasteless for a good portion of its depth. Those who like well-done steak are gastronomically on the wrong side of the fence and generally incorrigible. It is not necessary, however, to make them unhappy. Broil their steak for as long as it takes to satisfy them—its terminal state, after all, is really none of your affair.

Experiment with *your* stove; find out *its* time and stick to it. Let no cookbook thereafter mislead you.

SERVE WITH: Just about anything. French fries are classic with steak, whether at home or abroad. Nonetheless, they are a nuisance to prepare at home. GRILLED POTATOES (p. 34)—my standby—are easier and better. As a change from potatoes in any form, spaghetti with a home-brewed tomato sauce (p. 34) is more than welcome.

SERVINGS: Steak servings depend on weight—and how much weight, per person, depends on how much steak that person can consume. In spite of the great American dream of an 18 oz. portion, I think ¾ lb., trimmed weight, is adequate for almost anyone. This may be acquired in individual steaks or in one large steak, provided that it does not make the steak too thick. When serving more than one from a large steak, slice the steak into diagnoal strips ¾″ to 1″ wide, depending on the area of the steak.

My wife and I, jointly and severally, are a bug on this. Food is not only as good as it tastes, but as good as it looks. Don't slap the steak on the plate with its juices slobbering over the side. Place it attractively. Use a napkin to wipe

off the drippings. Pre-wash a few sprigs of parsley or watercress and pop them on your platter before serving. It is no trouble and will enable your family to experience the illusion of elegant dining.

SHALLOT BUTTER

1 lb. butter
½ cup shallots, finely chopped
½ cup parsley, finely chopped
1 tbsp. salt
1 tbsp. black pepper

1. Let the butter soften at room temperature. When it is soft enough to manipulate, knead the other ingredients into it until they are evenly distributed throughout the butter.

2. Re-form the butter into four rolls, the diameter of a half-dollar. Wrap them in waxed paper and chill.

PRE-PREPARATION: These rolls of SHALLOT BUTTER may be constituted for freezer storage and kept indefinitely. There is, therefore, no need to wait for *the* steak night to prepare it.

3. Before serving, cut as many ¼ inch slices as are required. Place one on each steak after you remove it from the broiler.

SERVINGS: About 90 pats—a pound will cover a multitude of steaks.

GRILLED POTATOES À LA MODE DE MA FEMME

Peel and cut potatoes into strips about half as thick as for French fries. Dry them well. Place them in a broiler pan. Dot them, liberally, with butter or other shortening. Sprinkle with salt, pepper and paprika. Broil, at least 4 inches from the flame, until tender, stirring occasionally to coat the potatoes with the shortening and the seasoning and to permit all to become browned. It will require 20 to 30 minutes of cooking time. The result is a crisper, tastier, less greasy version of French fried potatoes. As an interesting innovation, grill sweet potatoes in the same way. These are a perfect complement to CHICKEN HAMBURGERS À LA MODE DE MA FEMME (p. 57).

SERVINGS: Figure 1½ potatoes per person, unless the potatoes are gigantic. These go fast and endlessly, like peanuts.

SPAGHETTI SAUCE À LA MODE DE MA FEMME

4 tbsps. olive oil
½ lb. chopped beef (optional)
2 onions, chopped
2 cloves garlic, sliced
2 tbsps. parsley, chopped
2 1 lb. cans Italian plum tomatoes
½ 6 oz. can Italian tomato paste

salt, pepper, sugar to taste
crushed red pepper to taste

1. Heat the oil in a saucepan.

2. If meat is used, crumble it into the hot oil and sauté it for 10 minutes, until it is brown. Add the onion, garlic and parsley and sauté for 5 minutes longer. If meat is not used, sauté the vegetables, alone, in the hot oil.

3. Add the tomatoes, tomato paste and seasonings. Cook at a boil for 5 minutes. Lower the flame to a minimum. Simmer for 1 hour.

PRE-PREPARATION: The sauce may be cooked in advance and re-heated before serving. In fact, it may be cooked whenever you choose and frozen—as may any leftovers.

SERVINGS: Depending on your taste, this recipe is far and away enough for 1 lb. of spaghetti. How much spaghetti, again depends on how much spaghetti you can take. In our home, 4 to 6 could gorge on it.

MARINATED STEAK, NORTH ITALIAN STYLE

steak or steaks, depending on weight, as for BROILED STEAK (p. 31), cut 1½″ thick
6 tbsps. olive oil
2 tbsps. parsley, chopped
2 cloves garlic, crushed
2 tsps. lemon juice

1. Mix the oil, parsley, garlic and lemon juice to form a marinade.

2. Brush the steak on all sides with, and let it remain in, the marinade for 2 hours, turning once.

3. Drain and broil, as you would any other steak, to the desired state of doneness.

SERVE WITH: Any of the garnitures suggested for BROILED STEAK (p. 32).

The French, popular mythology to the contrary, consume as many biftecks *and* pommes frites *as we do—but never* as *we do. They prefer the pan to the flame, and, as far as food is concerned, the French are not really ever wrong. The sauté process evokes the flavor in the meat that sheer broiling suppresses. Sautéed steak is plain meat,* oui, *but not on the hoof.*

SAUTÉED STEAK

- steak or steaks, depending on weight, as for BROILED STEAK (p. 31), cut under, but not over, ¾″ thick
- 1 tbsp. butter

1. Melt the butter in a skillet and heat it.

2. Place the steak in the hot butter and cook it over high heat for 2 minutes on each side, or until it is brown.

Reduce the heat and continue to sauté until it is done to taste.

3. Season and serve. If you wish to be adventurous without getting caught, heat a clove of garlic or brown a sliced onion in the butter—and remove it—before adding the meat. No one will be the wiser, but the flavor of your steak will be marvelously enhanced.

SERVE WITH: Anything that goes with steak.

A pan is per se *an invitation to a pan sauce. Without gumming up your nice clean steak, it will elevate its flavor to recognized gourmet heights. Some pan sauces are made with the meat still in the pan; others just after its removal. Their variety is profuse and, with imagination, can be infinite. For your maiden efforts, we suggest one of the "before" sauces and one of the "after."*

SAUTÉED STEAK WITH SHALLOT SAUCE

steak, as for SAUTÉED STEAK (p. 36)
4 tbsps. butter
6 shallots, chopped (or 1 small onion and ½ clove garlic)
½ cup dry red wine
salt and pepper to taste

1. Melt 2 tbsps. of the butter in a skillet and in it sauté the steak as for SAUTÉED STEAK (p. 36).

2. Salt and pepper the steak and remove it to a heated platter.

3. Add the remaining 2 tbsps. of butter to the pan. Raise the flame and quickly brown the shallots. Remove the pan from the fire and, immediately, stir in the wine, scraping in all of the brown bits around the pan. Re-heat gently, if need be, and pour the sauce over the steak. The whole works should not require more than 2 minutes.

SAUTÉED STEAK WITH MADEIRA SAUCE

6 tbsps. butter
2 onions, thinly sliced
steak, as for SAUTÉED STEAK (p. 36)
salt and pepper to taste
½ cup Madeira (or Sherry—it's cheaper)
4 tbsps. hot water

1. Melt 4 tbsps. of the butter in a skillet. Add the onions and sauté them until they are golden. Remove them from the pan with a slotted spoon.

2. Add the steak and cook it over high heat for 2 minutes on each side, or until brown.

3. Quickly return the onions to the pan, add the salt and pepper, the remaining 2 tbsps. of the butter, the Madeira or Sherry and the hot water. Lower the flame and continue to cook the steak until done to taste, turning once. Serve the steak with the sauce poured over it.

We do not serve left-over steak at the Cookery; we do not have any. At home, it is either wasted, or ingested as cold shoe leather, i.e. *in any home but mine. My wife, of course, makes it worth eating. Her recipe is equally adaptable to left-over roast beef or boiled beef. It produces a* plat *that stands so much on its own as to obscure completely its left-over origins.*

LEFT-OVER STEAK SAUTÉ

¾ lb. (more or less) left-over beef
1 tbsp. butter
1 onion, chopped
¼ tsp. salt
dash of ground black pepper
¼ cup bouillon
⅓ cup dry white wine
1 clove garlic, crushed
1 tbsp. parsley, chopped

1. Slice the beef as thinly as possible. Melt the butter in a skillet. Add the beef, onion, salt and pepper. Sauté until the beef slices are brown on both sides. Add the bouillon, wine, garlic and parsley.
2. Simmer until there is barely any sauce left.

SERVE WITH: Finely puréed mashed potatoes and little green peas, *petit pois,* which have been heated with a lump of butter.

SERVINGS: Serves somewhat less than 4, but the likelihood of your having more left-over meat than that is slight—so stretch it the best way you can.

That flavorful, full-blooded and inexpensive cut of meat, the "hanger" or "butcher's tenderloin" can be used, as we have mentioned, to enrich a menu in many ways. Methods of preparing it are legion. Let ours give you a hint—you take it from there. Nota Bene: *It is not a criminal offense, as we have also mentioned, to produce the suggested dishes with the more expensive steak cuts—or even filet mignon, if life has been good to you.*

BROILED TENDERLOIN STEAK

1½ lbs. butcher's tenderloin

Cut the butcher's tenderloin lengthwise, along the center tendon, and remove it. Butterfly each of the two strips of meat with which you are left, *i.e.* cut them through, almost completely, so that the meat strips will open like a book—or like a butterfly's wings in flight. Broil these tenderloin steaks as you would any other steak, but keep them on the rare side.

SERVE WITH: Anything that strikes you as appropriate for steak, for this, too, is steak.

PAN-FRIED TENDERLOIN STEAK

1½ lbs. butcher's tenderloin
3 medium onions, sliced
2 tbsps. butter
salt, pepper, paprika

1. Prepare the butcher's tenderloin as for BROILED TENDERLOIN STEAK (p. 40).

2. Melt the butter in a skillet. Add the onions. Sprinkle with salt, pepper and paprika to taste. Then, sauté the onions slowly until they are soft and golden. Remove them from the pan and keep them warm.

3. Raise the flame. Add the steak portions and sear them on both sides. Reduce the flame and continue to cook them until they are done to taste, turning once.

SERVE WITH: The natural pan juices; smother with the sautéed onions. Oddly enough, there is nothing that tastes better with this than plain, ordinary mashed potatoes and a green vegetable, if you insist, like a sour pickle.

TENDERLOIN STEAK SANDWICH

1 lb. butcher's tenderloin

Prepare the butcher's tenderloin as for BROILED TENDERLOIN STEAK (p. 40), but do not butterfly the halves.

Broil each half whole, allowing more broiling time because of the double thickness of the meat. Slice the broiled meat in ½ inch diagonal slices and lay the slices, by portions, on buttered toast. Toasted rounds of French or Italian bread are better.

SERVE WITH: Relishes to your taste, and plain or with SAUCE MAISON (below) as we do. Mustard sauce or a sauce diable are fine, too.

SAUCE MAISON

1 tbsp. flour
1 tbsp. butter
1 cup stock or water
1 tbsp. onion, finely chopped
½ small clove garlic, crushed
1 tbsp. oil
¼ tsp. dry mustard
2 tsps. Worcestershire sauce
½ tsp. Maggi seasoning
1 tbsp. parsley, finely chopped

1. Melt the butter in a saucepan. Remove it from the fire. Add the flour to the butter, blending it in until there are no lumps. Return the pan to the stove and stir the mixture, over a low flame, until it is the color of a brown paper bag. Again remove the pan from the flame. Bit by bit, add the stock or water, again taking care to eliminate all lumps. Return the pan to the stove once more, stirring the mixture constantly until it begins to thicken. Cook it over a low flame stirring occasionally, for 20 minutes. This pro-

duces a simple, although not very classic, *Sauce Espagnole,* the traditional base of any brown sauce.

2. In another pan, cook the onion and garlic in the oil, until the vegetables are soft.

3. Mix together the mustard, Worcestershire sauce and Maggi seasoning.

4. When the *Sauce Espagnole* is ready, stir in the sautéed vegetables and the spices. Simmer 5 minutes longer to amalgamate the flavors. Add the chopped parsley.

PRE-PREPARATION: The sauce may be made in advance and re-heated before use.

SERVINGS: The recipe will produce approximately 1 cup of sauce, which is a proper amount for 4 steak sandwiches.

TENDERLOIN OF BEEF, CHINESE STYLE

1½ lbs. butcher's tenderloin
4 tbsps. oil
½ clove garlic, mashed
½ tsp. pepper
1 tsp. salt
½ tsp. sugar
¼ tsp. powdered ginger
1 1 lb. can bean sprouts
2 tomatoes, quartered
2 green peppers, cut in 1½″ pieces
4 tbsps. soy sauce
¼ cup cold water
3 tbsps. corn starch
3 scallions, cut in ¼″ pieces

[*A tip on Chinese cookery:* Chinese food must be cooked quickly and immediately before eating—it cannot be kept waiting. Yet, it requires substantial pre-preparation because of the number of ingredients involved. Therefore do all of your cutting, slicing, mixing, etc., before you start to cook. Line up the measured and prepared ingredients in the order that they are to go into the pan. The actual cooking then becomes a simple belt-line operation: from preparation board to pot—to table.]

1. Trim the butcher's tenderloin as for BROILED TENDERLOIN STEAK (p. 40). Leaving each half whole, cut it on the diagonal, into paper thin slices. Mash the garlic; measure out the salt, pepper, sugar and ginger. Wash and drain the canned bean sprouts; cut the tomatoes and green peppers as required. In a cup, mix, until smooth, the soy sauce, water and corn starch. Chop the scallions.

> PRE-PREPARATION: If step "1" is not done in advance, you may as well give up in advance.

2. NOW: heat the oil in a large skillet. Add the garlic, salt, pepper, sugar and ginger. Add the sliced meat. Cook it over a brisk flame, stirring so that the meat browns on all sides. When it is almost done, cover the pan and cook it for 2 minutes more. Remove the beef from the pan and reserve. Unless you do this, the meat will become soft and flavorless.

3. Add to the pan the bean sprouts, tomatoes and green peppers. Cook them for about 5 minutes, stirring often. The vegetables will be crisp in the Chinese manner. If this offends you, cook them until they are soft enough for you, but the result will be neither Chinese nor good—the way my husband likes them.

4. Return the meat to the pan with the vegetables. Stir the cornstarch mixture into the meat and vegetable mixture. Stirring constantly, cook until the sauce is thickened. It usually takes 2 or 3 minutes more.

5. Turn into a serving dish and sprinkle with the chopped scallions.

6. Yes, I know; but it only seems that way. It is really a very simple, fast dish to make. Do all of your preparation work early in the day so that, by dinner time, you will have forgotten about its rigors. The cooking time, then, will be no more than 20 minutes, positively guaranteed.

SERVE WITH: Rice, of course. Hot mustard, which you prepare by mixing dry mustard with water, adds a nice bite.

TENDERLOIN OF BEEF, RUSSIAN STYLE, TO WIT: STROGANOV

1½ lbs. butcher's tenderloin
2 onions, chopped
3 tbsps. butter
1 tbsp. flour
¾ cup sour cream
1 tbsp. chili sauce
Tabasco sauce, to taste

1. Trim the butcher's tenderloin as for BROILED TENDERLOIN STEAK (p. 40). Leaving each half whole, cut them, on the diagonal, into ½ inch slices.

2. Melt the butter and, in it, sauté the onions for about 2 minutes. Add the meat, season it with salt and pepper and sauté it for 5 or 6 minutes, turning the slices so that they brown on both sides. Sprinkle the flour over the meat and continue to sauté for 2 or 3 minutes longer, stirring occasionally.

3. Add the sour cream and cook until the contents of the pan are hot again, but do not permit them to boil. Add the chili sauce, Tabasco and more salt, to taste. Stir, and it is ready for the table.

SERVE WITH: BOEUF STROGANOV is classically accompanied by fried or oven-browned potatoes and over-cooked mixed vegetables, but you do not have to make a fetish about what is classical.

TENDERLOIN OF BEEF, TAHITIAN STYLE

1½ lbs. butcher's tenderloin
3 tbsps. butter
1 green pepper, cut in 1″ pieces

1 large onion, cut in 1" cubes
4 large mushrooms, sliced
4 water chestnuts, sliced in rounds
salt, pepper, monosodium glutamate (commonly sold as MSG or Acc'ent), to taste
1 tomato, peeled, seeded and quartered
2 tbsps. Claret
1 tbsp. Bovril
1 tbsp. soy sauce

1. Prepare the butcher's tenderloin as for BROILED TENDERLOIN STEAK (p. 40). Leaving each half whole, slice them, on the diagonal, into ½ inch slices.

2. Melt the butter in a skillet and, in it, sauté the green pepper, onion, mushrooms and water chestnuts until they are tender, but still crisp. Season the vegetables with salt, pepper and MSG. Add the tomato.

3. Grease another skillet lightly and, in it, brown the meat slices over high heat.

4. Mix the Claret, Bovril and soy sauce.

PRE-PREPARATION: This dish may be made in advance to this point, provided the three mixtures are stored separately until the final step is taken.

5. Combine the meat strips with the vegetables in a skillet. Heat quickly. Stir in the Claret-Bovril-soy sauce mixture. Cook until all of the ingredients are thoroughly heated and the meat is done as you like it.

SERVE WITH: Rice. In Oriental-type meals, it is quite possible to escape the inevitable vegetables and/or salad. Take advantage of this. Give them a Rum-soaked pineapple, instead, for dessert.

Chuck is an economical cut of meat that takes some doing to make really palatable. My wife does, indeed, and with an ease that struggling chuck consumers will well appreciate. The dish is even better made with a sirloin steak, which need not be of top quality because of the long cooking time to which it is subjected.

BAKED CHUCK STEAK À LA MODE DE MA FEMME

1 1½ lb. chuck steak
2 medium onions, sliced
2 green peppers, cut in ⅛s
2 large tomatoes, cut in ⅛s
½ cup ketchup, diluted with ¼ cup water
salt, pepper

1. Trim as much fat as possible from the chuck steak. Place it in a shallow baking pan and slip it under a hot broiler flame for 5 minutes on each side, to brown. Drain any fat accumulated in the pan.

2. Pepper and salt the steak. Scatter the prepared vegetables over the top of the steak.

PRE-PREPARATION: The baked steak may be pre-prepared in advance thus far, if it is of any use to you. In any event, its pre-preparation presents no pre-dinner rush. It is a mere matter of transferring it from the oven to the table.

3. Pour the diluted ketchup over the meat and vegetables. Place the pan in a 350 degree oven for at least 1½ hours, basting occasionally with the juices in the pan. Should too much of the liquid evaporate, add more di-

luted ketchup. Serve, cut in broad diagonal slices, topped with the vegetables and moistened with the liquid remaining in the pan.

SERVE WITH: Par-boiled small potatoes or quartered large ones, which have been placed in the pan an hour before the dish is done and basted with the pan juices.

CHOPPED BEEFSTEAK

2 lbs. good chopped beef

We are of the school of thought that chopped steak should be made from meat and meat alone. Any flavoring ought to come from the outside, and only after it is cooked. As with steak, it is good meat that makes a good chopped steak. Excellent for this purpose is the "tail" of the porterhouse or shell steak, sirloin and, again, butcher's tenderloin. Have the meat well trimmed before it is ground. Do not handle it much and do not pack it hard when shaping it. Mold it gently into short thick loaves, weighing about ½ lb. each. Broil until done to your taste. The time, of course, depends on the heat of your stove and the thickness of the loaf you have made. If it is chopped steak that you want, this is it. Adulterated—whether for good or for evil—it is a misbegotten meat loaf, which, we suppose, does have a place in a free society: for those who are just crazy to have indigestion.

PLANKED CHOPPED BEEFSTEAK

2 lbs. potatoes
1 tsp. salt
white pepper to taste
2 eggs, slightly beaten
2 egg yolks
2 lbs. chopped beef, prepared as for CHOPPED BEEFSTEAK (p. 49)
4 wooden cooking planks
1 small tomato, quartered
8 mushroom caps
cooked green peas (optional)
cooked string beans, cut (optional)
cooked asparagus tips (optional)
2 tbsps. butter, melted

1. Peel, cut and cook the potatoes in lightly salted water until they are tender. Drain them and dry them by returning them to the fire, over high heat, until the last of the cooking water has evaporated—about 30 seconds. Mash or rice the potatoes. Add the salt, pepper, eggs and egg yolks. Mix these ingredients thoroughly. The product is known, culinarily, as POMMES DUCHESSE.
2. Prepare the steaks.
3. Prepare the vegetables you choose to use.

PRE-PREPARATION: These basic items of the PLANKED CHOPPED BEEFSTEAK may be prepared in advance.

4. Broil the steaks for the time required to finish cooking one side. Turn them and place each of them, raw side up on a separate wooden cooking plank. With a

pastry tube, make a border of the potatoes around the steak. For each portion, press into the potato border, ¼ tomato, 2 mushroom caps, and, if you choose, a bouquet of string beans, a mound of peas and two or three asparagus tips. The garnish should, of course, form an appealing decorative whole. Brush the exposed parts of the potato border with the melted butter. Dribble some on the vegetables as well.

5. Return the filled plank to the broiler and continue the broiling until the steak is done to your liking. The potatoes, by that time, should be brown and the vegetables hot.

6. Garnish the plank with parsley.

SERVE WITH: A mixed green salad to complement the vegetables, which are an integral part of the dish.

CHOPPED BEEFSTEAK ROQUEFORT

5 oz. Roquefort cheese
2 tbsps. cream
2 tbsps. onion, finely chopped
⅛ tsp. garlic, crushed
1 tsp. Worcestershire sauce
¼ tsp. black pepper
2 lbs. chopped beef, prepared as for CHOPPED BEEFSTEAK (p. 49)

1. Knead together all of the ingredients, except the chopped beef, until they form a smooth creamy mixture.

2. Prepare the steaks.

PRE-PREPARATION: This work may be done in advance.

3. Broil the steaks until they are done on one side. Turn them and broil them on the other side for approximately half the time required to complete their cooking to your taste.

4. Remove the steaks from the broiler and spread each with ¼ of the cheese mixture. Return them to the broiler until they are done. By then, the cheese will be nicely melted and slightly brown. If you prefer a lesser coating of cheese, suit your own desires: this recipe is quite heavy handed and may offend you unless you are truly a Roquefort buff.

SERVE WITH: GRILLED POTATOES À LA MODE DE MA FEMME (p. 34) and a mixed salad, which includes tomato—mildly French-dressed, naturally. The Roquefort flavor is too powerful to bear competition.

CHOPPED BEEFSTEAK À LA MIRABEAU

2 lbs. chopped beef, prepared as for CHOPPED BEEFSTEAK (p. 49)
anchovy butter
48 flat anchovy filets
48 slices of pimento stuffed green olives

1. Prepare the steaks and broil them until they are done on one side.

2. Turn them and brush their raw sides with anchovy butter.

3. Lay six strips of anchovies, in a lattice pattern, on each steak. In each of the interstices formed by the anchovy strips, place a slice of the olives.

4. Return the steaks to the broiler and continue to broil them until they are done to your taste.

SERVE WITH: Any accompaniment suitable for steak, but choose bland, rather than spicy ones, to avoid conflict with the MIRABEAU flavors.

CHOPPED BEEFSTEAK PARMIGIANA

2 cups of either SPAGHETTI SAUCE À LA MODE DE MA FEMME (p. 34) or the sauce for LA PIPÉRADE (p. 110)
2 lbs. chopped beef, prepared as for CHOPPED BEEFSTEAK (p. 49)
4 1/8″ slices of Mozzarella cheese

1. Prepare the sauce of your choice.
2. Prepare the steaks.

PRE-PREPARATION: This is preliminary work, which may be done ahead.

3. Broil the steaks until they are done on one side. Turn them and broil them long enough to sear the top surface on the other side. Remove them from the broiler.

4. Spread the top of each steak with ½ cup of the sauce. Place one slice of Mozzarella cheese over the sauce

on each steak and return the garnished steaks to the broiler. Broil them until the steaks are done to your taste and the cheese is melted and lightly browned.

SERVE WITH: A salad and crisp loaf of Italian bread. If you must have a starch, try POTATO BALLS (below).

POTATO BALLS

1 recipe POMME DUCHESSE, as for PLANKED CHOPPED BEEFSTEAK (p. 50)
bread crumbs

1. Prepare the potatoes.
2. Form the potatoes into balls the size of a walnut. Roll them in bread crumbs. Brown them on a greased pan in a 450 degree oven for 15 minutes or until golden brown.

CHOPPED BEEFSTEAK À CHEVAL

2 lbs. chopped beef, prepared as for CHOPPED BEEFSTEAK (p. 49)
4 eggs
8 flat filets of anchovies
capers

1. Prepare and broil the steaks.
2. A few minutes before the steaks are ready, fry each of the eggs, separately.

3. Upon removing the steaks from the broiler, place a fried egg upon each and upon each yolk, cross 2 anchovy filets. Sprinkle with capers.

SERVE WITH: Mashed potatoes, a green vegetable, and a favorite of mine TOMATO AND ONION SALAD (below).

TOMATO AND ONION SALAD

2 large ripe tomatoes, cut in 1/8s
1 small onion, thinly sliced
1 recipe FRENCH DRESSING À LA MODE D'ANNE-MARIE (p. 162)

1. Combine all of the ingredients.
2. If you have the time, permit the salad to marinate, under refrigeration, for at least 1 hour before serving it. This is one salad which improves with the passage of time: its flavors blend and mellow; its limpness, unlike with greens, adds to its palatability.

CHOPPED BEEFSTEAK ROYAL HAWAIIAN

8 strips of bacon
2 lbs. chopped beef, prepared as for CHOPPED BEEFSTEAK (p. 49)
4 tbsps. Duk sauce or its equivalent
2 bananas, cut in 1/2 lengthwise
2 tbsps. butter, melted

1. Pre-cook the bacon until much of its fat is rendered, but it is still limp.

2. Broil the steaks until they are done on one side. Turn them and broil them long enough to sear the top surface of the other side.

3. Spread the newly seared surface of each steak with 1 tbsp. of the Duk sauce (available, bottled, in most supermarkets). Drop 2 strips of the limp bacon over each steak and top the whole with ½ banana. Brush each of the banana halves with ½ tbsp. of the melted butter.

4. Broil the steaks until they are done to your taste. The bacon will by then have crisped, and the bananas browned.

SERVE WITH: RICE PILAF WITH RAISINS AND NUTS (p. 30) and VINEGAR COLE SLAW (p. 159). Potatoes, in any form, go well, of course, but its Royal Hawaiian-ness seems to call for something a bit more exotic.

Hamburgers—on a bun—are equally amenable to the treatment the Cookery affords chopped beefsteaks. To convert an ordinary barbecue or midnight supper into a startling culinary event, serve your hamburgers in one of the styles suggested for chopped beefsteak. Better still, prepare some of each of the garnishes and let your guests make their own choice. The risk is: a toll of six hamburgers per guest.

BEEFBURGERS

1 lb. good chopped beef

A hamburger—a good one that is—is a chopped steak but half the size.

SERVE WITH: Need we mention that it may be served with pickles and onions, both?

À propos *of the subject of hamburgers, my wife—who else?—suggested we recommend a chicken hamburger. It is a nice variation of both chicken and hamburger and, simple though it is, it has an epicurean air.*

CHICKEN HAMBURGERS À LA MODE DE MA FEMME

1 3 lb. chicken, skinned and boned
1 medium onion
1 carrot
1 tbsp. bread crumbs
1 egg
2 tbsps. butter
pinch of dry mustard
touch of Tabasco sauce

1. Grind the chicken, onion, carrot and butter. Add the remaining ingredients and mix lightly.

2. Form the mixture into patties about the size and shape of a hamburger. Coat the patties lightly with additional bread crumbs.

PRE-PREPARATION: The hamburgers may be made up as indicated and stored in the refrigerator until they are to be broiled.

3. Sprinkle the prepared hamburgers with additional melted butter and broil, 4 inches from the flame, for about 10 minutes on each side or until cooked through. Sprinkle the newly exposed side with melted butter upon turning. The hamburgers may also be sautéed, but they are not quite as good that way.

SERVE WITH: The hamburgers are neutral enough in flavor to accept any garnish. We like them with GRILLED (SWEET) POTATOES À LA MODE DE MA FEMME (p. 34) and stewed tomatoes or lima beans.

SERVINGS: Serves 4, if you divide the mixture into enough patties. Figure 2 chicken hamburgers to a portion.

HAM STEAK HAWAIIAN

4 ¾" boned, pre-cooked ham steaks
4 tbsps. Duk sauce
4 slices canned pineapple
4 tbsps. red currant jelly

1. This ham steak can be made either in a skillet, under a broiler or on a grill. In any event, it must be finished under a broiler flame.

2. Score the rind of the ham steak to prevent curling. Cook it until it is nicely brown on one side. Turn. If you are broiling it, spread the uncooked side of each steak lightly with 1 tbsp. of the Duk sauce; if you are using a skillet or a grill, put the Duk sauce on the browned side. Top each steak with a pineapple slice and fill its hole with the jelly. Cook until the bottom side of the steak is browned. Transfer the pan to a broiler until the Duk sauce and jelly have completely melted and glazed the upper surfaces of the steaks.

SERVE WITH: Baked or candied sweet potatoes or fried white potatoes and CREAMY COLE SLAW À LA MODE DE MA FEMME (p. 159).

The thing about tartar steak that distinguishes it from all of the other recipes in this chapter is that it is neither broiled nor grilled. In fact, it is totally and completely uncooked, to wit: raw. All of its vitamins and minerals, we are told, remain intact and, we suppose, that is a virtue. If you are a tartar steak fan or propose to enjoy its benefits, we guess our way of preparing this raw meat "delicacy" is about as engaging as any. It does, we know, have its devotees.

TARTAR STEAK

2 lbs. of the finest beef you can buy
4 raw egg yolks
anchovy filets
capers
chopped hard-cooked egg
chopped raw onion

1. Trim the beef to within an inch of its life. The only fat that should remain is the internal graining of the meat. Grind the trimmed meat. Form it gently into ½ lb. loaves as for CHOPPED BEEFSTEAK (p. 49).

2. To serve, make an indentation in the top of each loaf of beef. Place the raw egg yolk in the indentation. Garnish with anchovy filets and capers. Surround with mounds of chopped hard-cooked egg and chopped raw onion. Pass the pepper mill and salt.

To establish, once again, the ingenuity of man and his capacity to devise an exception to every rule, a former Cookery cook originated a cooked *tartar steak, if you please, a veritable contradiction in terms. In fact, he created two versions: one that is good and one that he likes better. The principle, however, remains the same. Cooked or not, the tartar steak is still raw meat!*

CROQUE TARTARE

12 slices of white bread, trimmed
24 oz. of chopped beef, as for TARTAR STEAK (p. 60)
4 eggs, beaten with 4 tbsps. milk
shortening for deep frying

1. Spread 4 oz. of the beef on each of 6 slices of the white bread. Cover each with the remaining slices of white bread, *i.e.* make a sandwich. Cut each sandwich in half, not on the diagonal, but to form two oblongs. The portion should be three halves per person.

2. Dip the sandwiches into the beaten egg, saturating them well. Fry them in the deep fat until the bread is golden brown.

3. The answer to the riddle is: in the time it takes the bread to brown, the meat inside will not even begin to cook. It will remain raw, to wit: tartar steak.

SERVE WITH: A criss-cross of anchovy filets and capers on each sandwich half or spicy condiments of your choice.

CROQUE TARTARE EXTRAORDINAIRE

24 oz. chopped beef, as for TARTAR STEAK (p. 60)
1½ tsps. thyme
1½ tsps. Tabasco sauce
1½ tsps. salt
1½ tsps. pepper
¼ cup finely minced onion

12 slices white bread, trimmed
4 eggs beaten with 4 tbsps. milk
shortening for deep frying

1. Mix, lightly, the meat and the seasonings.

2. Prepare and cook as prescribed for CROQUE TARTARE (p. 61).

For those who do not like TARTAR STEAK, *the cooked version has within it, also, the virtue, if it is cooked long enough, of converting the raw meat into cooked meat. The result: a French-toasted beefburger, unusual and good.*

– a lonely roast

ARE ROAST BEEF is great. The Cookery does not serve it.

Nothing less than prime prime-ribs—sliced thick, at that—is really roast beef. Nothing more than something less can be made available at the Cookery's modest prices.

Roast lamb, like all lamb, is commonly just tolerated by the man on the street, although he may be compelled to eat it at home.

Roast veal is usually segregated with lamb.

Pork is risky.

And pot roast—who does not have that all too often?

I love my wife. She came up with the rarest of roasts for the Cookery, the only one we serve, and we are the only ones who serve it: CORNED BEEF FOURRÉ VIRGINIE. It is as beautiful as it is unique as it is simple to prepare. And, in addition, it tastes good.

CORNED BEEF FOURRÉ VIRGINIE

Corned brisket of beef (as much as you need)
½ tbsp. mixed pickling spice, per lb.
½ clove garlic, peeled, per lb.
whole cloves
brown sugar

1. Place the corned beef in water to cover and bring it to a boil. Pour off the water. Fill the pot with fresh water and again bring it to a boil. Reduce the heat to a bare simmer. Add the pickling spice and garlic. Cover the pot, partially, and continue to simmer until the beef is tender, but not mushy, approximately 50 minutes per pound. Replace the water as it evaporates, during cooking. Drain the corned beef and cool it until you can handle it or until you are ready to prepare it further.

2. Place the corned beef in an open baking pan. Stud it, in even rows, with whole cloves. Pack the top with brown sugar.

3. Moisten the sugar packing, ever so slightly, for, if you pour the liquid on, it will wash the sugar away. Pour some of the liquid into the pan as well. Bake in a 350 degree oven for about 45 minutes, basting occasionally with the carmelized pan juices. If the glaze develops bald spots in the course of baking, pat some additional brown sugar on the spots with a spoon and moisten them gently. Esthetically, you should end up with a glistening surface over all.

SERVE WITH: Pineapple slices—stick a maraschino in the hole—which have been baked in the same pan as the corned beef, and baked sweet potatoes. Or, baked beans and CREAMY COLE SLAW À LA MODE DE MA FEMME (p. 159). If you decide on the pineapple slices, use the juice in the can as the basting liquid for your roast.

SERVINGS: Since corned beef shrinks incredibly in the boiling, it is recommended that you allow at least ¾ lb. per person.

CORNED BEEF HASH

2 cups cooked corned beef, finely chopped
½ green pepper, finely chopped
2 cups cooked potatoes, ground
1 small onion, ground
1 egg
pepper, cayenne
butter or other shortening

1. Chop the corned beef and the green pepper. Put the potatoes (left-overs are fine) and onion through a meat grinder at its coarsest setting. Add the egg and seasoning to the other ingredients and mix lightly but thoroughly.

2. Form the mixture into long flat cakes about the size of two hamburgers put together.

3. Fry the hash cakes in a skillet in butter or other shortening until brown on both sides.

SERVE WITH: Something spicy, like pickled beets, or refreshing, like our VINEGAR COLE SLAW (p. 159).

I must say that my wife's pot roast is extraordinary. I feel compelled to offer her recipe as a public service to the afflicted generations of a pot roast culture, whereof the memory of man runneth not to the contrary. My wife, in her unstrained generosity, has added her formulae for a species of soft corn fritters and a potato kugel, *now third generation on her mother's side—both perfect with the pot roast's natural gravy. Nor shall I, with the common weal in mind, withhold my single, though masterful, culinary success: potato pancakes. To confess, I got the recipe from my brother who got it from a man who was the best potato pancake maker in Moscow. In this hoped for era of peaceful co-existence, I suppose I may be permitted to say: these potato pancakes are the best in the world.*

POT ROAST OF BEEF À LA MODE DE MA FEMME

Brisket of beef (as much as you need)
1 onion, chopped, for each lb. of meat
1 tomato, quartered (or ½ cup canned) for each lb. of meat
1 clove of garlic, peeled, for each lb. of meat
salt, pepper, paprika

1. Use a heavy dutch oven, if possible. Place it on the fire and turn the gas jet up as high as it will go. Put the meat in the pot and sear it on all sides.

2. Add the chopped onion. Reduce the heat somewhat and continue to cook until the onions have softened a bit. Sprinkle salt, pepper and paprika over the onions and

the exposed surface of the brisket. Add the garlic and tomatoes. Cover the pot and turn the flame down as low as possible. Cook for 15 minutes. Turn the meat and sprinkle salt, pepper and paprika over the newly exposed meat surface. Continue to do this until all of the meat's facets have been seasoned. Then let it settle down to serious cooking, at the same low heat, until tender, about 50 minutes to the pound. If you do not go to a movie in the interim, turn the meat every half hour or so. It cooks more evenly and the flavor improves. I do not, however, approve of rabid devotion to this principle. After all, of what purpose is a pot roast in the life of man—generic sense—if not to make possible a matinée?

PRE-PREPARATION: The pot roast may be made earlier in the day or even a day ahead, if you store the meat and gravy separately. In fact, there is a distinct advantage to cooking it in advance. Any fat in the gravy will congeal, on refrigeration, and may be removed easily.

SERVE WITH: My husband touts CORN FRITTERS (below), POTATO KUGEL (p. 70) or *his* POTATO PANCAKES (p. 71). However, since dinner comes at the end of a day—and so does fatigue—if you want a simpler accessory, just drop some small, whole potatoes—peeled, of course—into the pot roast about 1 hour before the end of the cooking time. Apple sauce, as a second side dish, sets off the flavor of the roast and *any* of its accompaniments.

SERVINGS: Particularly if you use brisket, it is wise to allow ¾ lb., raw meat, per person; perhaps slightly less, if you use rump or, banish the thought, chuck.

CORN FRITTERS

1 scant cup flour
2 eggs

1 1 lb. can creamed corn
1 tsp. salt
butter or shortening

1. Break the eggs. Mix the flour into the eggs, a little at a time, until you have a kind of sticky dough. Add the corn and the salt. Stir until the dough is well distributed through the corn. If you have time, let the batter stand for at least ½ hour.

2. Melt the butter in a skillet. Drop the batter, by tablespoons-full, into the pan and fry until each fritter is delicately brown on both sides. If you keep another pan hot over a very low flame, you can flip the finished pancakes into it to retain their warmth, while you fry the remaining batter.

SERVINGS: That much batter should serve 4, but the two of us usually finish it without help. These fritters, by the way, are also good, as a snack, with grilled bacon or ham and maple syrup.

POTATO KUGEL

4 large potatoes, grated
starch from the potatoes
1 onion, grated
1 egg, beaten
1 tbsp. bread crumbs
2 tbsps. melted butter or other shortening (chicken fat is superb!)
salt and white pepper to taste

1. Peel and grate the potatoes. Press the grated potatoes through a sieve, allowing the liquid to drain into a bowl. Let the liquid stand for 2 or 3 minutes and pour it away. On the bottom of the bowl, there will remain a layer of potato starch. Add this to the grated potatoes. Add the remaining ingredients and mix gently, but thoroughly. This operation should be performed as quickly as possible because, until at least the egg is added, the grated potatoes will begin to turn black.

2. Turn the batter into a greased baking dish, large enough for you to pat it down to a thickness of no more than ¾ of an inch; this will insure the KUGEL's outer crispness and avert its remaining soggy inside. Bake it in a 350 degree oven for 1 hour. Depending on the particular potato, the top may sometimes not brown enough; if so, place it under a broiler flame until it is colored to your taste.

PRE-PREPARATION: If you want to avoid the mess of preparing the KUGEL immediately before dinner, prepare and bake it half way, *i.e.*, for ½ hour, earlier in the day and finish the baking process before serving. The purpose of the half-baking is to assure that the potatoes in the KUGEL do not turn black.

SERVINGS: It should serve 4, but do not be surprised if it does not.

POTATO PANCAKES MOSCOVITE À LA MODE DE MON MARI

4 large potatoes, *un*peeled
1 small onion, grated

1 egg, beaten
4 tbsps. flour
salt and pepper to taste
vegetable shortening for frying

1. Scrub the potatoes well with a brush. Grate them, unpeeled, into a bowl. Add the grated onion, egg, flour and seasoning.

2. Heat 1 inch of shortening in a heavy skillet.

3. Using a large, perforated kitchen spoon, dip up a scoop of the potato batter, letting the accumulated liquid drain off, and lay it into the hot fat. Flatten it a bit in the pan. Repeat until the skillet is filled with pancakes. As you wait for those in the pan to brown, dip off and discard the liquid which forms in the mixing bowl. Keep frying the pancakes, turning them occasionally until they are a deep rich brown. Transfer them to a heated pan while you fry the next batch.

SERVINGS: I have no idea of how many this recipe serves. It is never enough. Once four of us—three of whom I shanghaied into grating—downed a batch made from 5 lbs. of potatoes—together with 6 lbs. of pot roast. I can only say, try it once for yourself, and, if you can establish some reasonable standard, please be guided by it.

Simple though it seems, I consider the inscription of this recipe a triumph of science over metaphysics. With my wife's help, my occult "feel" for the ingredients involved were translated into the material language of "tbsps." I am certain that even the Moscovite will appreciate that the final calibration of his chef d'oeuvre *for the use of the masses is, indeed, an historic event.* Alitur vitium vivitque tegendo.*

* If you are curious, it was Vergil who said it and he meant: "Vice is nourished by secrecy," and, it is fair to imply, vice versa.

from the casseroles

CASSEROLES CAME to the Cookery at the instigation of its customers and by the inspiration of my wife. The Cookery had opened originally, some decade and a half ago, as a simple, if uncommon—and uncommonly nice—hamburger restaurant. Its design was unorthodox in its artistry. Its service was unaccustomed in its felicity. Its food was singular in its quality and appeal. Its prices fit the average purse. The hamburger, in its less than infinite variety—with a few odds and ends for the alimentary oddballs—was the comestible keystone to this rare configuration of restaurant gratifications. Pleasures and prices, as had been anticipated, delighted to the point, as had not been anticipated, of too much return. The hamburger transient became the man who came to dinner—too often to be content with chopped steak alone. The *mot d'ordre* was: same place, same price *and* variety.

My wife's notion was to exploit the special genius of the average French *paysanne,* Italian *contadina,* Chinese 農夫, or Hawaiian *wakune.* Like us, they had invented low cost meals—of necessity—and, in doing it, created some of the world's most exquisite dishes. We did, in fact, decide to rob Pierre to feed our patrons. Ever since, simmering casseroles have greeted our guests and the air of the Cookery has been redolent with their pungent aromas.

i. chicken casseroles

POULET MARENGO

1 2½ lb. broiler
flour
salt, pepper
1 tbsp. oil
1 tbsp. butter
1 large clove garlic, finely chopped
1 *bouquet garni*
½ cup dry white wine
1 tbsp. brandy
1 large canned tomato, cut in pieces
1 cup mushrooms, quartered

1. Cut the chicken into serving pieces. Roll them lightly in flour, which has been seasoned with salt and

pepper. Heat the oil and butter in a skillet and, in it, brown the chicken, over an active flame, until it is golden on all sides. Transfer the chicken to a casserole.

2. To the chicken, add the garlic. Make a *bouquet garni* by tying together, with a string, half a stalk of celery, a few sprigs of parsley, sprinkled with a pinch of thyme, and a bay leaf. [So-called *bouquets garnis* may be purchased commercially in little tea bags, but these are so strong as to be overpowering.] Add the *bouquet* to the casserole.

PRE-PREPARATION: Thus far and no further.

3. Pour the wine and brandy into the casserole. Add the tomato pieces. Cover the casserole tightly and cook, gently, over a low flame, for 30 minutes, turning the chicken pieces occasionally. Add salt and pepper to taste and the mushrooms. Cook for 15 minutes longer or until the mushrooms are tender.

SERVE WITH: Rice, buttered toast points, as garnish, and a green salad.

SERVINGS: I am of the school that holds a single chicken serves 2—in a pinch, 3. Most people, I must concede, believe it serves 4.

Veal (about 1½ lbs.), cut in chunks, can be prepared in the same way for the equally classic VEAU SAUTÉ MARENGO.

POULET ESTEVAN

3 cups cooked chicken, chunked
3 tbsps. scallions, chopped

3 tbsps. butter
¾ cup canned water chestnuts, sliced
1 tsp. fresh ginger root, chopped, or ¼ tsp. powdered ginger
1½ cups sour cream

1. Melt the butter. Add the scallions and cook, slowly, until they are soft and golden. Add the chicken, water chestnuts and ginger. Mix gently, in order not to crumble the chicken.

PRE-PREPARATION: May be done to this point. The rest is a mere nothing.

2. Add the sour cream. Heat thoroughly, but do not boil.

SERVE WITH: Rice and a nice green salad—French dressing, of course.

CHICKEN EN CAPILOTADE

1 2½ lb. chicken, boiled
½ onion, chopped
1 tbsp. butter
1 tsp. flour
½ cup dry white wine
1 tsp. Bovril
1 cup hot water
½ cup canned tomato soup, undiluted
1 tbsp. parsley, chopped
pinch of nutmeg
1 cup mushrooms, sliced

1. Skin and bone the chicken and cut it into large chunks. Or, use, instead, left-over chicken or turkey; it makes a new dish out of an old fowl.

2. Cook the chopped onion in butter until soft but not brown. Sprinkle the flour over the onion and stir until blended. Add the wine. Stir until smooth. Dissolve the Bovril in the hot water and add it to the pan. Add all of the remaining ingredients, except the mushrooms, and cook over a moderate flame for 20 minutes.

PRE-PREPARATION: The chicken and the sauce may be made in advance and stored separately until used.

3. Combine the chicken, the sauce and the mushrooms and cook for 20 minutes, or until the mushrooms are tender.

SERVE WITH: Rice and a mixed green salad.

POLLO ALLA CACCIATORE

1 2½ lb. chicken
salt, pepper
flour
5 tbsps. olive oil
2 large onions, sliced
2 cloves garlic, sliced
1 cup canned tomatoes
1 cup mushrooms, sliced
1 large green pepper, sliced lengthwise
½ 6 oz. can tomato paste

1. Cut the chicken into serving pieces. Add the salt and pepper to the flour and roll the chicken parts in this

seasoned flour. Heat the oil in a skillet and, in it, brown the chicken, about 5 minutes on each side.

PRE-PREPARATION: It is best to stop advance preparation here.

2. Mix the onions, garlic, green peppers and canned tomatoes and add them to the chicken. Cover the skillet and simmer slowly for 20 minutes.

PRE-PREPARATION: Advance preparation can also be continued to here, but it tends to be less good.

3. Add the mushrooms and continue to cook for an additional 15 minutes, or until the mushrooms are soft.

PRE-PREPARATION: If you want to be as free as a bird before serving time, it is possible to cook it all ahead and merely re-heat before use. However, not only will the chicken seem less fresh, but the mushrooms will be mushy.

SERVE WITH: Rice or fettucine, *i.e.*, broad egg noodles, salad and plenty of fresh Italian bread.

POH LOH KAI

1 2½ lb. chicken
flour
1 egg, beaten with 2 tbsps. water
bread crumbs
shortening for frying
1 tbsp. oil
1 cup pineapple juice
1 tbsp. corn starch
6 tbsps. water
3 tbsps. vinegar

1 tbsp. soy sauce
½ cup brown sugar
¼ cup ketchup
3 green peppers, cut in 1½″ chunks
1 cup pineapple chunks, fresh, frozen or canned
½ cup maraschino cherries
¾ cup sweet mixed pickles

1. Cut the chicken into about 20 pieces, as for RUMAKI (p. 28). Dip the pieces in flour, then in egg and then in bread crumbs. Fry, until well browned, either in deep or shallow shortening. Drain on paper toweling and reserve. [If ever you have the inclination to make this dish more luxurious, skin and bone the chicken, coat it with a fritter batter and fry the pieces in deep fat—but you have to be either a really dedicated cook or slightly mad to do it.]

2. In a large saucepan, heat the oil and pineapple juice. In a separate dish, mix the cornstarch and water until smooth. Add this mixture to the pineapple juice mixture. Also add the vinegar, soy sauce, brown sugar and ketchup. Cook until the sauce begins to thicken, stirring constantly.

PRE-PREPARATION: These first two processes may be done way in advance of meal time—and the mess cleaned up.

3. Add the green peppers to the sauce and simmer 10 minutes. Add the remaining ingredients and the fried chicken. Stir and heat thoroughly, remembering, both in stirring and serving, to treat the chicken gently so as not to crumble its coating.

SERVE WITH: Rice. If you are afraid of going hungry, serve a first course and a dessert.

KENTUCKY BURGOO

1 5 lb. fowl
5 qts. water
1 cup frozen okra, sliced
1 cup frozen peas
1 cup kernel corn, canned or frozen
1 cup frozen cut green beans
½ cup dried lima beans
2 large potatoes, cubed
2 large carrots, sliced
2 tbsps. salt
1 tsp. pepper
1 stalk celery
2 green peppers, chopped
2 large onions, chopped
1 1 lb. head cabbage, shredded
3 whole cloves
2 whole cloves garlic
3 1 lb. cans tomatoes
2 tbsps. Worcestershire sauce
¼ cup chili sauce

1. Put all of the ingredients, except the chicken and the 5 qts. of water, into a LARGE pot or kettle. Bring it to a boil, reduce the flame and simmer for 1 hour, stirring occasionally.

2. Place the fowl in a separate pot with the 5 qts. of water. Bring it to a boil. Remove and disjoint the chicken. Save the water. Then wait for step "1" to be completed.

3. Put the disjointed chicken, together with the liquid in which it boiled, into the vegetable-spice mixture. Cover the kettle partially and cook until the fowl is done, ap-

proximately 3 hours, over a slow fire. Serve in deep soup plates.

PRE-PREPARATION: I see no reason why the BURGOO cannot be cooked completely and re-heated. Remember, though, that it will take a considerable amount of time to make such a mess of stuff hot again.

SERVE WITH: A ladle of rice atop each portion and sprinkled with crumbled strips of crisply broiled bacon.

SERVINGS: This recipe serves at least 8. To proportion it for 4 would necessitate using a young 2½ lb. fryer, which, unlike a large fowl, could not, without falling to shreds, take the long cooking time required to give the BURGOO flavor. Just reserve BURGOO for a big crowd.

The BURGOO *is, despite its many components, a very simple recipe. You merely keep throwing things into the pot as their names jump up on the list. It may take a good pitching arm, but very little culinary skill.*

POULE-AU-POT HENRI IV

1 3 lb. chicken, with the giblets (except for the liver), quartered
3 quarts of water
2 medium onions, whole
1 large stalk celery
4 small carrots, whole
2 tbsps. salt
2 cups cooked rice

1. Clean the chicken well. Peel the onions and carrots and wash them and the celery thoroughly. Place all of the ingredients, except the rice, in a large pot. Bring it to a boil. Skim off any scum which may rise to the surface. Reduce the heat until the pot is just barely bubbling and continue to cook, partly covered, for 1½ hours or until the chicken is tender.

2. Discard the onions and celery. Add the rice to the pot and cook for a few minutes until the whole is hot again.

SERVE WITH: That with which it was cooked. Place, *en casserole,* or in a deep soup bowl, for each person, ¼ chicken and a carrot, covered with the soup-rice mixture. Some call this boiled chicken-in-the-pot—and they are not wrong.

SERVINGS: If you use the chicken to serve only 2, the balance of the soup may be used the next day as a first course. Add some shredded lettuce, during the re-warming process, and let your guests add soy sauce to their taste. It will provide a delicate change of flavor.

LOBSTER AND CHICKEN GUMBO

1 3 lb. chicken, cut in pieces
5 tbsps. butter
1 large onion, sliced
1 large clove garlic, sliced
½ cup celery, chopped
1 1 lb. can tomatoes
½ lb. frozen okra, sliced

1 bay leaf
½ tsp. powdered thyme
pinch of cayenne
salt and pepper to taste
1 quart boiling water
½ lb. fresh picked lobster meat—or, indeed, the more the merrier

1. In 2 tbsps. of the butter, brown the chicken pieces lightly and reserve them.

2. Melt the remaining butter in a deep pot, a dutch oven, if possible. Sauté the onion, garlic and celery in the butter for 10 minutes. Add the tomatoes, okra, bay leaf, thyme, salt, pepper and cayenne to taste. Stir well and gradually add the boiling water. Simmer for 15 minutes.

PRE-PREPARATION: It is best to stop here.

3. Add the browned chicken to the vegetable mixture and simmer slowly for 40 minutes longer.

PRE-PREPARATION: Or here.

3. Remove 1 cup of clear broth from the gumbo pot, and, in a separate pan, heat the lobster chunks in the broth for about 10 minutes.

PRE-PREPARATION: But certainly, don't work it to here. The lobster will suffer from the additional cooking of the re-heating process.

4. Serve in casseroles or deep soup plates, apportioning the chicken-vegetable-broth mixture and topping each portion with about 2 oz. of the heated lobster meat. If you feel really flush, try it with all-lobster meat—about 1 lb.: prepare the sauce as in step "2" above, but let it cook for 40 minutes; add the lobster for 10 minutes of cooking. Al-

ways remember, as I have said, not to overcook the lobster. If you do, it will toughen and become tasteless.

SERVE WITH: Boiled rice may be served either on the side or placed on the bottom of the serving bowl, and the gumbo poured over it. This is a soupy kind of meal and requires nothing but bread and cheese and coffee to end it.

LOBSTER AND CHICKEN CREOLE VIEUX CARRÉ

1 3 lb. chicken, cut in pieces
5 tbsps. butter
2 small onions, finely chopped
2 green peppers, chopped
1 clove garlic, finely chopped
1 1 lb. can tomatoes
½ 6 oz. can tomato paste
1 tsp. paprika
salt and pepper to taste
½ lb. fresh picked lobster meat—or as much as you can afford

1. In 2 tbsps. of the butter, sauté the chicken pieces until they are lightly browned. Remove the chicken and reserve.

2. Melt the remaining butter and, in it, sauté the onions, green peppers and garlic until soft, but not brown. Add the tomatoes, tomato paste, paprika, salt and pepper. Simmer for 10 minutes.

PRE-PREPARATION: To here only.

3. Add the browned chicken to the vegetables. Cover and simmer slowly for 30 minutes.

PRE-PREPARATION: To here, if pressed.

4. Add the lobster meat to the pan and continue to simmer for 10 minutes more, until thoroughly heated.

PRE-PREPARATION: You are through! Re-heat no more!

SERVE WITH: Rice. There are enough vegetables in the creole sauce. Serve a salad, if it makes you feel virtuous.

ii. beef casseroles

MANDARIN MEATBALLS

1½ lbs. ground beef
1 egg
1½ tbsps. corn starch
1½ tsps. salt
3 tbsps. onion, chopped
freshly ground black pepper
1½ tbsps. oil
POH LOH KAI sauce (p. 80)

1. Mix, *very lightly,* the beef, egg, cornstarch, onion, salt and pepper. Form the mixture into walnut-sized balls and brown them in the oil.

2. Prepare the POH LOH KAI sauce.

PRE-PREPARATION: Cook ahead to this point, without fear, keeping the meat balls and the sauce separate.

3. Cook the meat balls in the sauce for 15 minutes.

SERVE WITH: Rice.

BOLLITO

3 lbs. beef flanken (short ribs will do, if you have no choice)
2 medium onions, whole
4 small carrots, whole
1 stalk celery
3 qts. water or to cover
1½ cups dried lima beans
2 tbsps. salt

1. Wash the dried lima beans and soak them in water to cover for 1 hour.

2. Have the butcher cut your meat, not with the ribs as for short ribs, but across the rib in strips about 3 inches long. For 3 lbs., you will probably get two long cross-rib strips, which you then cut into serving portions, each containing one or two bones.

3. Place the meat in a colander and pour boiling water over it, so that each surface of each piece turns a light gray. This seals in the blood and juices and prevents a dirty looking soup.

4. Peel and wash the vegetables well.

5. Place all of the ingredients in a deep pot and bring them to a boil. Skim off any scum that forms. Partially cover the pot and simmer, so that the liquid barely bubbles, for about 2¾ hours, or until the beef and beans are tender.

PRE-PREPARATION: Prepare it entirely ahead, but store the meat and other solids separately from the soup.

SERVE WITH: Its pot-mates. *En casserole* or in a deep soup plate, apportion, for each person, a carrot, an adequate amount of meat, beans and soup. Accompany with prepared grated horseradish. At home, we like to eat our soup first, with boiled barley, and the meat, beans and carrots as a separate course. When sauerkraut—fresh out of the barrel—is in season (early winter), we really live.

SERVINGS: Serves 4 more than adequately. Left-over soup is excellent when re-heated, garnished differently for variety. Try any excess beef as LEFT-OVER STEAK SAUTÉ (p. 39).

My wife's mother—who, in matters of cooking as in other things, defies all the traditions of being a mother-in-law —passed on to my wife from her mother, who was an old Odessa-nik, the perfect recipe for a real Russian cabbage borscht. The same cut of meat is used as for BOLLITO, *but it provides a hearty culinary break—temporary, if you insist—from the foods of the Anglo-Saxon West. It generates a warmth, on a cold winter's night, with which the more common heating devices of modern man cannot compete.*

RUSSIAN CABBAGE BORSCHT

3 lbs. beef flanken or short ribs
water barely to cover
1 large head of cabbage, shredded as for cole slaw
2 large onions, coarsely chopped
2 1 lb. cans tomatoes
2 tbsps. salt
1 infinitely small piece of sour salt (or lemon, if you must substitute)

1. You will need a LARGE pot.

2. Have the beef cut and scalded as for BOLLITO (p. 85). Place it in the pot with the water. Bring it to a boil and skim the scum that forms.

3. Add the remaining ingredients. Bring the pot to a boil again, turn the heat as low as possible and cook for 2 or 3 hours. The borscht takes on flavor as it cooks. It also requires tasting as it cooks. Start this process after it has cooked for about an hour. It should have a nice tart taste, but not so sour as to shrivel your mouth. To adjust the flavor, work carefully with salt, sugar and sour salt. Beware of the sour salt, however; it is potent, and a small piece goes a long way.

PRE-PREPARATION: The more you cook this BORSCHT, the better it tastes. It is, therefore, a natural for advance cooking.

SERVE WITH: A whole boiled potato, added to each soup bowl on serving, to make this meal-in-one seem more balanced. That addition is not strictly Russian, but it does have its purpose.

SERVINGS: By Russian standards, it will serve 4, but, insofar as BORSCHT is concerned, they can take it.

Flanken, like butcher's tenderloin, is another of my wife's nostrums. She can find more things to do with it than an Escoffier can with filet mignon—for which our budget is much obliged. It does undoubtedly adapt itself well to soups, converting them into effortless one-dish meals. I understand that the younger generation, my wife not included, has no notion that soup comes from anywhere but a can. Yet, if you would be disposed to concoct a BOLLITO *or a* BORSCHT, *I suggest you consider, as well, my wife's be-flankened tomato or vegetable soups. Some marinated herring first, a tossed green salad to follow, a beautiful* brie *and fruit to bring up the rear, and you've catered a feast with no work at all.*

TOMATO-SOUP-NOT-OUT-OF-A-CAN À LA MODE DE MA FEMME

3 lbs. flanken or short ribs
water barely to cover
2 large onions, whole
2 tbsps. salt

2 1 lb. cans stewed tomatoes
¼ tsp. sugar
3 tbsps. raw rice, washed
1 green pepper, cut in julienne

1. Have the beef cut and scalded as for BOLLITO (p. 88). Place it in a pot with the water, the onions and the salt. Bring it to a boil and skim the scum that forms.

2. Add the tomatoes and the sugar. Cover the pot partially, bring it to boiling, lower the flame and simmer for 1¾ hours, or until the beef is all but tender.

3. Remove the beef. Put the remaining contents of the pot through a strainer or food mill, forcing through as much of the tomato and onion pulp as possible. You should be able to sieve almost everything but the tomato seeds.

4. Return the beef to the pot with the strained soup, the rice, and the green pepper. Cover the pot partially again and cook slowly, stirring occasionally, for at least 30 minutes more, certainly until the rice is soft.

5. Taste the soup, from time to time, during cooking. It should have a rich tomato flavor. If it is lackluster, it takes either salt, sugar or both to bring out its fullness. When you hit it right, you will know, but do not use your remembrance of the taste of the canned stuff as a guide. It will have no relation to that—it will taste like tomato soup.

PRE-PREPARATION: This soup takes well to reheating. It may even be frozen for future use without loss of zing. Therefore, it matters not when you cook it, so long as you do.

SERVINGS: It will serve 4 as a meal with meat in it, and, in addition, at least 4 more as a soup course.

VEGETABLE SOUP, WITHOUT-A-DOUBT, À LA MODE DE MA FEMME

3 lbs. flanken or short ribs
water to cover
2 large onions, whole
1 stalk celery
2 tbsps. salt
½ cup split peas, washed
¼ cup barley, well washed
½ cup dried lima beans, washed
4 carrots, diced
1 1 lb. can stewed tomatoes
1 pkg. frozen string beans
1 pkg. frozen lima beans
1 8 oz. can green peas
1 8 oz. can kernel corn

1. Have the beef cut and scalded as for BOLLITO (p. 88). Place it in a pot, with water to cover together with the onions, celery, salt, split peas, barley, dried lima beans and carrots. Bring the whole to a boil and skim the scum, which forms, from the top. Add the tomatoes. Reduce the heat to the point where the soup barely bubbles. Simmer for 1½ hours, with the pot partially covered.

2. Add the frozen string beans and lima beans. Cover the pot partially and simmer for 1 hour more.

3. Add the canned peas and corn, with their liquid. Taste for seasoning and heat thoroughly. Serve portions of the meat and soup in casseroles or deep bowls.

PRE-PREPARATION: This soup, too, takes well to

re-heating. It may be made any time and used any time thereafter.

SERVINGS: Serves 4 with meat and, in addition, at least 4 more as a meatless soup.

MANZO ALLA MODA

1½ lbs. stewing beef, well trimmed, cut in chunks
6 tbsps. olive oil
1 large onion, chopped
1 large clove garlic, sliced
1 cup mushrooms, sliced
½ green pepper, chopped
½ cup canned tomatoes
½ cup dry red wine
¼ tsp. oregano
½ tsp. basil
salt and pepper to taste

1. Heat 2 tbsps. of the oil in a skillet, and, in it, brown the meat chunks on all sides. Remove and place them in a deep casserole.

2. Add the remaining oil to the skillet, heat it, and, in it, sauté the onions, garlic, mushrooms and green pepper until tender, but not brown. Remove the vegetables and add them to the casserole with the meat.

3. Stir in the tomatoes, wine and spices. Simmer the casserole, covered, for 2 hours.

PRE-PREPARATION: Make it all in advance, if you choose, and re-heat.

SERVE WITH: Pasta, in some form, or rice. Sometimes, as here, salad seems to be the only other proper course.

PANHANDLE POTTAGE

1 lb. ground beef
3 tbsps. butter
1 1 lb. can tomatoes
2 carrots, sliced
1 onion, chopped
1 green pepper, chopped
½ cup celery, chopped
2 tbsps. salt
1 tsp. chili powder
¼ tsp. pepper
¼ cup barley, washed
2½ cups chicken broth
2 cups potatoes, diced

1. Crumble the meat and brown it in the butter in a large casserole. Add the other ingredients, except for the potatoes. Cover and simmer for 1¼ hours.

2. Add the potatoes. Cover and simmer for ¾ hour longer, making certain that the potatoes are soft.

PRE-PREPARATION: It may be made wholly in advance and re-heated. Take care in storing it, however, since chopped meat spoils rapidly.

SERVE WITH: A French-dressed green salad. All the other vegetables are internal.

CASSEROLE DE BOEUF PYRÉNÉENNE

1½ lbs. stewing beef, chunked
3 tbsps. butter

3 onions, chopped
2 cloves garlic, crushed
½ cup cooked ham, diced
salt and pepper
bouquet garni
¾ cup hot water
¾ cup dry white wine
2 green peppers, cut in 1″ pieces

1. Melt the butter in a heavy casserole or dutch oven. Brown the meat chunks. Add the onions, garlic, ham and salt and pepper to taste.

2. Make a *bouquet garni* by sprinkling several sprigs of parsley with powdered thyme and tying them together with a bay leaf. Add the *bouquet* to the casserole.

3. Add the water and the wine. Cover the pot tightly and cook the beef in a 250 degree oven for about 2½ hours. After 2 hours, add the green pepper and re-cover until the cooking is finished.

SERVE WITH: Rice and TOMATO AND ONION SALAD (p. 55).

CASSEROLE DE BOEUF BOURGUIGNONNE

1½ lbs. stewing beef, chunked
3 tbsps. butter
2 onions, chopped
2 carrots, cut in large pieces
1 clove garlic, finely chopped
2 shallots, finely chopped (optional, but good)
1 tbsp. flour

salt and pepper to taste
1½ cups red wine
1 cup water or stock
1 *bouquet garni*
¼ cup Sherry
½ lb. mushrooms, caps whole, stems sliced in rounds (optional)

1. Heat the butter in a heavy casserole and, in it, brown the beef pieces well, until they are a deep mahogany in color. This is the essence of a good BOEUF BOURGUIGNON. Remove the beef from the pan.

2. To the pan in which the beef has browned, add the additional tbsp. of butter and the onions, garlic and shallots. Brown them lightly.

3. Return the beef to the pan. Sprinkle the meat and vegetables with the flour, the salt and the pepper. Mix thoroughly. Add the wine and the water or stock. The liquids should just barely cover the meat. If they do not, add water until it is. Add a *bouquet garni* made by tying together 1 stalk of celery, 3 sprigs of parsley, sprinkled with a bit of powdered thyme, and a bay leaf.

4. Cover the casserole tightly and simmer over the lowest possible flame for 2 hours. The beef should be fork tender and the sauce a deep rich brown.

PRE-PREPARATION: The casserole may be prepared to this point, either the same day or even the day before you plan to serve it.

5. Add the Sherry and the mushrooms. Cook for 45 minutes longer.

SERVE WITH: A green salad and crusty French bread to sop up the sauce. In this case, it pays to be French and happy rather than American-polite and deprived.

iii. veal casserole

VITELLO CON PEPERONI

1½ lbs. veal, chunked
3 tbsps. butter
2 cloves garlic, sliced
1 1 lb. can tomatoes
3 tbsps. tomato paste
salt and pepper to taste
1 large onion, sliced
4 green peppers, cut in 1″ strips
5 tbsps. olive oil
½ cup dry Sherry

1. Melt the butter in a skillet. Brown the garlic lightly. Add the veal chunks and sauté them until they are brown, about 10 minutes. Add salt and pepper to taste, the tomatoes and the tomato paste. Cover and simmer slowly for 30 minutes.

2. Fry the onions and peppers, in another pan, in the hot oil until they are soft.

PRE-PREPARATION: You may prepare in advance this far, but keep the meat mixture and the fried vegetables separate.

3. Combine the veal mixture and the vegetables. Add the Sherry. Cover the pan and simmer very slowly for 20 minutes longer.

SERVE WITH: Rice or pasta, salad and bread. A wedge of *Bel Paese* and a pear is perfect in conclusion.

iv. steam table division (if you'll excuse the expression)

The two items on the Cookery menus which have been with us from the first moment there was a Cookery—the small trial store opposite Bloomingdale's in New York—are the Cookery BEEF STEW and the Cookery MEXICOBURGER, a kind of stew on a bun, but H-O-T. Both of these, by our own admission against interest, are served from our kitchen's steam table. Yet, both were and are as popular as if a *maître d'* had made them before our guests' very eyes. The answer, of course, is not in our stars, but in our stews. A steam table is not *de rigueur*. A pot will do and the pleasure is all yours.

COOKERY BEEF STEW

2 lbs. stewing beef
2 tbsps. butter or other shortening
2 large onions, chopped
2 large carrots, diced
1 clove garlic, minced
1 tbsp. flour
1 tbsp. paprika
2 tbsps. salt
½ tsp. pepper
½ bay leaf
1 cup canned whole tomatoes

½ cup canned tomato sauce
½ cup water
8 small potatoes, whole, or 4 large ones, quartered
cooked mixed vegetables

1. Melt the shortening in a kettle or, if possible, a dutch oven. Brown the meat and remove it temporarily.

2. Add the onions and carrots to the fat remaining in the pot and cook them until they are golden.

3. Return the beef to the pot. Sprinkle the meat with the flour, paprika, salt and pepper. Mix well. Add all of the remaining ingredients, except the vegetables. Mix well. Cover tightly and cook slowly for at least 2 hours—3 is better.

PRE-PREPARATION: Cook it whenever you like. The capacity of stew to be re-heated is legendary.

4. An hour before the stew is done, add the potatoes. Turn it into a serving dish and garnish with the cooked mixed vegetables.

My wife is sometimes opinionated. Although it is a beef stew recipe developed by her that our customers like so well, she feels that it is a mere catering to taste that should be better developed. For a better stew, she says, sweet potatoes, rather than white, are a sine qua non. *Cooking the vegetables in the stew, rather than as garnish, she says, is simply a must. I just mention it in passing—and because she insisted. It is also true that the stews we eat at home have a special quality.*

COOKERY MEXICOBURGER

1½ lbs. stewing beef
water to cover
1 cup chili sauce
¼ cup vinegar
¼ cup brown sugar
1 tbsp. dry mustard
1 bay leaf
1 clove garlic, whole
½ tsp. Worcestershire sauce
⅛ tsp. Tabasco sauce
⅛ tsp. crushed red pepper
1 tbsp. oil

1. Put the meat in a deep kettle with water to cover. Boil it at a fast clip, adding water as the original water evaporates, until the meat is so soft as to be in shreds—about 2 hours. Drain the meat and shred it into fibers, removing all fat and connective tissue in the process.

2. While the meat is cooking, make the sauce by combining the remaining ingredients. Bring them to the boiling point, turn the flame low, and cook for 1 hour.

3. Mix the meat and sauce together in the following proportions: for every cup of shredded meat, add ¾ cup of sauce. Cook the mixture, slowly, for 30 minutes, until the meat takes on the sauce's flavors.

PRE-PREPARATION: We make it ahead, as a steam table item, and so, obviously, may you. Do not, however, combine the meat and the sauce until you are ready to heat it for service.

SERVE WITH: A toasted bun, as a sandwich, as does the Cookery. Or, for more of a meal, serve it over thin spaghetti, rice, or mashed potatoes. Have ready a nice, cool dessert, like sherbet.

SERVINGS: As a main course it will serve only 4, but as a sandwich it is adequate for 6.

With one of my wife's myriad food ideas, we filled another well in the steam table and thereby added two new dishes to our dinner menu: boiled tongue and/or baked ham in COOKERY RAISIN SAUCE. *Tongue, undoubtedly, is tongue, and ham is, undoubtedly, ditto. Yet, dressed with* COOKERY RAISIN SAUCE, *both have become meals of distinction at the Cookery.*

COOKERY RAISIN SAUCE

1 medium onion, chopped
1 tbsp. brown sugar
1 1 lb. can tomatoes, coarsely chopped
½ cup ketchup
½ tsp. salt
½ cup raisins

1. Place the onions and brown sugar in a large pan. Heat and stir until the sugar caramelizes around the onion pieces.
2. Add the remaining ingredients. Stir. Simmer, very

slowly, for 20 minutes.

PRE-PREPARATION: Make it all in advance; even freeze it, if you will.

SERVINGS: About 3 cups of sauce.

BEEF TONGUE, COOKERY RAISIN SAUCE

1 recipe COOKERY RAISIN SAUCE (p. 102)
1 2½ lb. pre-cooked beef tongue, or 1 4 lb. raw corned beef tongue

1. Prepare the sauce.

2. If you have purchased a pre-cooked tongue, which is readily available in any supermarket, half of your job is done. If you are like I am and prefer to suffer, boil the corned tongue in the manner suggested for the corned beef in CORNED BEEF FOURRÉ VIRGINIE (p. 66).

3. Slice the tongue—thick or thin, according to your preference. Heat the slices in the sauce until both are thoroughly hot and have exchanged flavors with each other.

4. To make this dish really elegant, use, instead of beef tongue, small, whole veal or lamb tongues. Parboil them for 1 hour, remove the skin, and cook them, slowly, for 1½ hours more in the COOKERY RAISIN SAUCE.

SERVE WITH: Rice or baked or mashed potatoes. Accompany with tossed green salad. A slice or two covered with sauce makes an excellent—and easy—first course, accompanied by nothing but bread.

VIRGINIA HAM, COOKERY RAISIN SAUCE

1 recipe COOKERY RAISIN SAUCE (p. 102)
2 lbs. pre-cooked ham, cut in slices ½″ thick

1. Prepare the sauce. Do not be mad enough to cook a ham. Just buy it and slice it.
2. Heat the slices of the ham in the sauce until they are heated through.

SERVE WITH: Any kind of potato, including baked sweet potato, or rice. Salad, sadly enough, seems to be the only other course that is fitting.

My wife also uses the COOKERY RAISIN SAUCE *as a base for stuffed cabbage—another way, incidentally, to use chopped meat that is neither a hamburger nor a meat ball.*

CABBAGE ROLLS, COOKERY RAISIN SAUCE

1 lb. chopped beef
1 tbsp. raw rice, washed
1 loosely packed head of cabbage
1½ recipes of COOKERY RAISIN SAUCE (p. 102)

1. Mix the rice, *lightly*, with the chopped beef.

2. Put the whole head of cabbage in a pot with water to cover. Bring it to a boil. Boil 5 minutes and remove the cabbage.

3. Cut the cabbage leaves at the base, near the core, and peel each leaf off the head.

4. Place a generous tablespoon of meat at the base of each leaf and roll, tucking in the ends so that the meat will not fall out. Use as many leaves as you have meat for. The balance of the head may be shredded, as for cole slaw, and added to the pot with the meat rolls.

5. Prepare the sauce. Heat it to a boil. Submerge the cabbage rolls in the boiling sauce. If the sauce does not seem to cover the rolls at first, be confident. It will, as the cabbage softens and collapses.

6. Reduce the flame to the lowest possible point. Cover the casserole and cook at least 3 hours. The longer the cooking, the better the flavor.

PRE-PREPARATION: Prepare it in advance and re-heat—the re-heating, like the long cooking, can only improve it, provided you recognize that there are limits to everything. The cabbage rolls may also be frozen.

SERVE WITH: Rice. Let this be an unbalanced meal. There is too much green in it to be able to face even a salad with it.

out of the frying pan

FOR ALL that there are grills, broiler racks, pots, kettles, and casseroles at the Cookery, the frying pans are always busy. With a few odd pans out, what they produce are: eggs.

Eggs are, in almost any cuisine but ours, a keystone of the epicurean *carte,* the province of the *chef de cuisine,* the *bonne bouche* of the gastronome. The endemic egg, unfortunately, is what a chicken lays, the estate of the short-order cook, the last refuge of the gastronomically irresolute. Boiled, poached, fried, scrambled, and, usually, murdered, they are eaten as habit for breakfast, from a poverty of ideas for lunch, and, in a calamity, for dinner. They often have little to recommend them but that they fill a void and are sanctioned, proverbially, as good in your beer.

Cookery patrons had always liked Cookery eggs. They were served to them any way they liked them but in their beer.* They were commendably prepared for their genre. They were the equal of any eggs in their class, and better than most. That, of course, was well enough, which we might well have left alone. But then, as I have said, I married. My wife's catholic culinary notions added egg *spécialités* to the Cookery menus above and beyond the call of American egg cookery. Our customers have not forsaken all other eggs, but they have, with a will, adopted our contributions to the local egg scene. For a luxurious Sunday breakfast, a midnight snack for the unexpected, or an evening when you do not feel like cooking, but do feel like eating, you, too, will welcome the Cookery's egg innovations.

i. scrambled, believe-it-or-not!

LA PIPÉRADE

2 tbsps. olive oil
2 green peppers, finely sliced
2 small onions, chopped
2 small cloves garlic, crushed
4 large canned tomatoes, drained, seeded and chopped
salt and pepper

* The Cookery does not serve beer.

2 tbsps. butter
8 eggs
4 slices ham or 8 slices Canadian bacon, grilled

1. In a large skillet, heat the oil and, in it, slowly sauté the green peppers, onions and garlic, salted and peppered to taste, until the onions are golden. Add the tomatoes and simmer for about 30 minutes, until the vegetables are truly soft.

PRE-PREPARATION: This vegetable mixture may be prepared in advance.

2. Beat the eggs lightly with salt and pepper.
3. Raise the flame to high under the vegetables. Add the butter. When the butter has melted, add the eggs and stir the eggs and vegetables together, constantly, until the eggs have reached a scrambled-egg type consistency to your liking.
4. Turn the eggs into a serving dish and top with the grilled ham or bacon, 1 slice of ham or 2 slices of bacon, per person.
5. It is best to prepare no more than 4 eggs at a time, using half the sauce each time. Eight eggs are not impossible, but just an awful lot to stir in one mass.

SERVE WITH: Crisp French bread, a tossed green salad —and a bottle of wine. French fried potatoes fill out the meal —although the French would be horrified.

SCOTCH WOODCOCK

8 eggs
8 tbsps. milk

4 tbsps. butter
16 anchovy filets
4 tbsps. capers
8 slices toast, buttered

1. Beat the eggs and milk and prepare scrambled eggs in the butter. Everybody does it wrong, *i.e.* fast. Eggs should be scrambled over the lowest possible flame and stirred constantly. It takes a long time to do it in this way—almost 15 minutes—but it is worth it. The product is creamy, fluffy, and rich—in sum, as compared to what usually passes for scrambled eggs, extraordinary.

2. Turn approximately 2 eggs on to 2 slices of the toast for each portion. Top each with a crisscross of four anchovy filets and 1 tbsp. of capers.

3. As with LA PIPÉRADE, scramble no more than 4 eggs at a time—for your own convenience.

OEUFS BROUILLÉS AUX FOIES DE VOLAILLES

(It sounds better in French, *s'il vous plaît*)

4 tbsps. butter
¼ cup onion or scallion, finely chopped
16 raw chicken livers, sliced
salt and pepper
8 eggs
8 tbsps. milk or cream

1. Melt the butter in a skillet. Add the chopped onion and sliced chicken livers and sauté them until the onions

are soft and golden and the livers are within a minute of being done.

2. Beat the eggs and milk (or cream) together. Add the mixture to the chicken liver pan. Scramble the eggs and liver mixture together until you have reached a desired state of scrambledness.

3. Turn the eggs onto a platter and surround them with toast points.

PRE-PREPARATION: Nothing may be prepared in advance. Neither liver nor eggs sit well.

SERVE WITH: Nothing, really, unless you are trying to stretch your meal. In that case, French fried potatoes and a salad.

ii. fried, indeed!

HUEVOS RANCHEROS

1 recipe of sauce for MEXICOBURGER (p. 101)
4 pancakes
8 sausages
4 eggs
4 tbsps. butter

1. Prepare the sauce and keep it hot. If you have prepared it in advance, heat it.

2. Cook the sausages and keep them warm.

3. Buy a nice pancake mix—*prego!*—and prepare 4 pancakes the size of an egg after it has been fried. Keep them warm on a serving platter large enough to hold them, in a slow oven. (If you choose to make your own pancake batter, you are on your own.)

4. Fry the eggs—one at a time—sunny side up. As each egg is cooked, slip it onto one of the pancakes.

5. When each pancake has been egged, remove the platter from the oven, pour sauce, in a quantity to your taste, over each egg, and surround the eggs with the sausages.

SERVINGS: With so rich a sauce and so much to go with it, it seems that 1 egg per portion is adequate. Should you disagree, double the number of eggs and the number of pancakes.

UOVA CON PROSCIUTTO E MOZZARELLA

8 2 oz. slices of cooked ham, cut ¼″ thick
4 slices of Mozzarella cheese, the size of the ham slice, cut ¼″ thick
2 eggs beaten with 2 tbsps. milk
flour
breadcrumbs
4 eggs

1. Sandwich 1 slice of the Mozzarella cheese between two slices of the ham. This will give you 4 ham-cheese sandwiches.

2. Pressing the ham-cheese sandwiches together, coat each of them with flour. Then dip each floured sandwich in the beaten eggs, and, after that, in the bread crumbs.

PRE-PREPARATION: Not only can these *beignets* be made in advance, but they should be: it helps set the breading.

3. Fry the coated ham-cheese sandwiches in either deep fat or butter until they are golden brown on both sides. Keep them warm in a slow oven while you prepare the eggs.

4. Fry each of the remaining 4 eggs, separately, sunny side up. Slip an egg on top of each *beignet*. Serve garnished with parsley.

SERVINGS: With a filling *beignet* underlying the egg, 1 egg per person should be enough of a portion. If it does not seem so to you, prepare 1 extra egg per serving.

HAWAIIAN HAM AND EGGS

4 2 oz. slices of ham, cut 1/4" thick
4 canned pineapple rings
2 tbsps. melted butter
20 cross-wise slices of banana
4 eggs

1. Grill the ham slices under a broiler. Top each slice with a pineapple ring and surmount the pineapple with five of the banana slices. Brush the fruit with the melted butter and continue to grill until the bananas are lightly brown. Keep warm while you prepare the eggs.

2. Fry each egg, individually, sunny side up. Place a fried egg on each ham pyramid. Serve garnished with watercress, if it is available; if not, with parsley.

SERVINGS: Double the recipe if you feel the one-egg portion is not adequate. It should be, however.

iii. poached, in a way!

EGGS BENEDICT

½ lb. butter
8 egg yolks
2 tbsps. lemon juice
white pepper and salt to taste (black pepper will dirty the sauce)
8 eggs
8 slices Canadian bacon
4 English muffins

1. Heat water in the bottom of a double-boiler, never letting it boil during the entire operation. In the top section, over the hot water, place the egg yolks and ¼ of the butter. Stir rapidly with a wire whisk or wooden spoon until the butter is melted. Then add another ¼ of the butter, stirring constantly until it has melted. Add the remainder of the butter, always stirring, until each piece is melted and the sauce thickens. Remove the top boiler pot

from the heat for several minutes and continue to beat it. Add the lemon juice, salt and pepper, and place the pot in the double-boiler again. Stir the sauce again, over the heat, for another minute or two.

When you have finished you will have HOLLANDAISE SAUCE, either beautiful or curdled, depending on your luck. It is a stinker of a sauce to make! I suggest you give up and try our EGGS BENEDICT MORNAY (below), which is just as good and less apt to disappoint.

2. Split and toast the English muffins. Grill the bacon. Poach the eggs.

3. Place the toasted muffins, open, in individual flat casseroles, 2 muffin halves to each dish. Place a slice of bacon on top of each half; place a poached egg over each bacon slice. Over all, pour the HOLLANDAISE SAUCE, in a quantity that suits you, but certainly to cover.

EGGS BENEDICT MORNAY

2 tbsps. butter
2 tbsps. flour
2 cups light cream, scalded with a slice of onion—put the onion in as you start to heat the milk
4 tbsps. grated Swiss or Parmesan cheese
8 eggs
8 slices Canadian bacon
4 English muffins

1. Melt the butter in a saucepan. Remove the pan from the fire. Stir in the flour. Add the scalded cream—discard the onion slice—and stir until smooth. Return the

pan to the fire and stir constantly—do not answer the telephone; let the baby cry—until the sauce thickens and comes to a boil. Boil, stirring constantly, for 2 minutes *on the clock.* Add the cheese; stir until it is melted into the sauce. This is a MORNAY SAUCE. Keep it warm over a double boiler or a flame-tamer.

PRE-PREPARATION: Actually, the MORNAY SAUCE can be made earlier in the day, kept well refrigerated, and reheated. It cannot, without real damage, be kept overnight.

2. Split and toast the English muffins. Grill the bacon. Poach the eggs.

3. Serve as you would EGGS BENEDICT (p. 116), but use the MORNAY SAUCE in place of the HOLLANDAISE SAUCE.

EGGS COLETTE

1 recipe MORNAY SAUCE, as for EGGS BENEDICT MORNAY (p. 117)
2 tbsps. butter
½ cup green pepper, cut in julienne
½ cup onions, finely chopped
1 cup mushrooms, sliced (optional)
1 tsp. salt
½ tsp. *white* pepper
2 cups cooked chicken, diced
2 canned pimentos, diced
1 cup *petit pois*
¼ cup Sherry
4 4 oz. pastry shells
4 eggs

1. Prepare the sauce. If you prefer creamed chicken without a cheese taste, eliminate the grated cheese from

the MORNAY SAUCE—you will then have made a *sauce blanche, i.e.*, a white sauce.

2. Melt the butter in a small skillet. In it, sauté the green pepper, onion and mushrooms, until they are soft. Add the salt and pepper.

3. Combine the sauce, the sautéed vegetables, the chicken, pimentos, and peas. Add the Sherry. Warm, without boiling, and keep warm while you prepare the eggs.

PRE-PREPARATION: This entire filling may be made ahead and re-warmed. It is best, however, not to add the Sherry until re-heating or it will evaporate.

4. Poach the eggs.

5. Fill each pastry shell ¾ full of the creamed chicken mixture and cover it with one of the poached eggs.

SERVINGS: Serve 1 filled shell per portion if you will. If this seems inadequate, simply buy 4 extra shells and poach 4 extra eggs.

EGGS CREOLE AU GRATIN

1 recipe of the sauce for LA PIPÉRADE (p. 110)
1 recipe MORNAY SAUCE, as for EGGS BENEDICT MORNAY (p. 117)
8 eggs

1. Prepare both required sauces, in advance if you wish. Heat them before you prepare the eggs.

2. Poach the eggs.

3. In individual boat-shaped serving dishes, place a layer of PIPÉRADE SAUCE. Set into the sauce, for each por-

tion, 2 poached eggs. Cover the eggs generously with MORNAY SAUCE. You can make it an even more pleasing looking dish if you trouble to sprinkle some grated cheese over the MORNAY SAUCE and brown it quickly under a high broiler flame.

UOVA ALLA CACCIATORE

1 recipe of the sauce for LA PIPÉRADE (p. 110)
4 tbsps. butter
16 raw chicken livers, sliced
8 eggs

1. Prepare the sauce and keep it hot.
2. Melt the butter in a skillet. Add the sliced chicken livers and sauté them until they are within a minute of being done. Add the PIPÉRADE SAUCE and cook the two, together, for a minute or two more. Keep warm—not for a long time—while you prepare the eggs.
3. Poach the eggs.
4. Place a generous amount of the sauce-liver mixture in each of 4 boat-shaped serving dishes. Into each dish set 2 of the poached eggs.

OEUFS BIGARADE

½ cup orange marmalade
½ cup canned tomato sauce
2 tbsps. lemon juice

8 orange slices, skinned
8 eggs

1. Mix together the marmalade, tomato sauce, and lemon juice. Heat thoroughly.

2. Place 2 orange slices in each of four individual serving dishes.

3. Poach the eggs.

4. Place a poached egg on each orange slice. Cover with a proportionate amount of the orange-tomato sauce.

iv. ah! omelets

We are firmly convinced that only the French can make omelets. The Russians make them like my grandmother; the Italians, like our beaneries; of the English, we will say nothing. What they do in Tahiti or Outer Mongolia, we do not know. But with the French, *omelette* making is a national art.

The Cookery omelets are not MADE IN FRANCE, but they are a reasonable facsimile thereof, both in quality and variety. In fact, they are merely fabulous. With a little practice—and a few flops—you should be able to do almost as well.

BASIC OMELET

2 eggs
salt and pepper
2 tbsps. water
½ tbsp. butter
1 7″ skillet

1. In a bowl, beat the eggs, seasonings and water.

2. Heat the butter in the skillet, over a bright flame, until it is hot, but not smoking. Add the eggs all at once. Pull the edges of the egg mass toward the center as they thicken. The still liquid egg will fill the vacant spaces. Keep pulling the edges until no liquid remains, but the whole must, in the end, be still soft.

3. Slide the omelet onto a serving plate until half is on the plate and half yet in the pan. Flip the half still in the pan onto the half in the plate, forming a half-moon shape.

4. To be really elegant, brush the top of the omelet with melted butter and put it under a hot broiler flame, for no more than a minute, to glaze.

SERVINGS: This recipe, being basic, serves 1. If you want to serve 4, make 4 of them—or two 4-egg omelets. The only thing that can be prepared "for 4" in relation to an omelet is the filling, if any. The omelet itself is an individual or semi-individual job.

OMELETTE À LA REINE

1 recipe of creamed chicken as for EGGS COLETTE (p. 118)
4 2-egg BASIC OMELETS (above) or 2 4-egg BASIC OMELETS

1. Prepare the creamed chicken.

2. Prepare the BASIC OMELETS, one at a time. Slide each onto a heat-proof serving dish, filling it with the creamed chicken, in the following manner. For each omelet, as you slide half the omelet onto your serving platter, spoon half of its portion of the creamed chicken filling onto the omelet half that is on the plate. Flip the other half of the omelet over the filling. Pour the remaining part of its portion of the creamed chicken onto the serving plate to surround the omelet. [My law partner, Blanch Freedman, who can fully understand a Felix Frankfurter decision, but whose brilliance is apparently confined to the complex, insists that she does not have enough hands to follow these instructions. To those who may be possessed of the same mental deficiency, I can only say: PUT THE PLATE DOWN on the table! That will leave you with the egg skillet in one hand and the sauce ladle in the other. Two hands.]

3. Sprinkle the omelets with grated Swiss or Parmesan cheese and slip them under a broiler flame—not for long—until the cheese melts.

SERVE WITH: Salad—that alone will do well—or buttered asparagus. French bread is a must; garlic bread adds to the overall flavor of the meal.

OMELETTE SAVOYARDE

2 4 oz. slices of cooked ham, or 4 2 oz. slices, cut 1/4" thick—depending on the number of omelets you make

2 4 oz. slices of Cheddar or American cheese, or 4 2 oz. slices, cut 1/4" thick

4 2-egg BASIC OMELETS (p. 122) or 2 4-egg BASIC OMELETS

1. Grill the ham. Prepare the omelets, keeping each omelet warm in a slow oven while preparing the others—but be quick about it, or the eggs will become rubbery.

2. Top each omelet with a slice of the grilled ham and top that with a slice of cheese. Slip them under a high broiler flame until the cheese melts. Garnish with parsley.

SERVE WITH: This omelet seems like one of those egg dishes that should be eaten *per se*. If a side dish is desired, however, some sort of salad is always good.

OMELETTE PAYSANNE

2 cups cubed fried potatoes
12 strips of bacon, cooked crisp
8 tbsps. water
8 eggs
2 tbsps. butter

1. Prepare the fried potatoes. Cook the bacon and cut it into ½ inch pieces.

2. Beat together the eggs and the water.

3. Add to the eggs, ½ cup of the fried potatoes for each 2 eggs and the equivalent of 3 strips of bacon. Mix thoroughly.

4. Fry and serve the egg-potato-bacon mixture in the same way you would a BASIC OMELET (p. 122). A watercress garnish is pleasant.

SERVE WITH: Nothing or anything but potatoes.

OMELETTE À LA RUSSE

4 2-egg BASIC OMELETS (p. 122) or 2 4-egg BASIC OMELETS
8 oz. sour cream
4 oz. red salmon roe caviar

1. Prepare the BASIC OMELETS, but with this difference: fold them in the real French manner. When you are ready to turn the omelet onto the serving dish, slide it, in the pan, back toward the handle and flip that back ⅓ of the omelet over on itself. Then fold the rest over onto the dish as you would a BASIC OMELET. The appearance will be that of a small jelly roll with the unseamed part on top.

2. Slit the top of the omelet lengthwise, and, into the slit in each of the omelets, for each 2 eggs, spoon 2 oz. of the sour cream. On top of the sour cream, for each 2 eggs, place 1 oz. of the red caviar.

SERVE WITH: Black bread and butter.

CHICKEN LIVER OMELET

4 tbsps. butter
12 small mushrooms, sliced
1 medium onion, minced (shallots are better—about 8)
16 raw chicken livers, sliced
salt and pepper
¼ cup Marsala or Sherry (optional, but good)
4 2-egg BASIC OMELETS (p. 122) or 2 4-egg BASIC OMELETS

1. Melt 2 tbsps. of the butter in a skillet. Add the mushrooms and onions and sauté them until they are soft.

Remove them from the pan and reserve.

2. Add the remaining 2 tbsps. of butter to the pan, raise the flame and brown the chicken livers quickly.

3. Return the mushrooms and the onions to the pan, add the seasoning and the wine, and simmer for 3 or 4 minutes more—do not overcook. Keep warm.

PRE-PREPARATION: This is one sauce that ought *not* to be prepared in advance. Chicken livers are never right unless cooked at the last moment.

4. Prepare the BASIC OMELETS one at a time. Fill each with a proportionate amount of the chicken liver mixture, in the manner prescribed for filling an OMELETTE À LA REINE (p. 122). If you are really afraid of making an omelet, pour the beaten eggs into the hot chicken liver mixture and scramble as for OEUFS BROUILLÉS AUX FOIES DE VOLAILLES (p. 112). It is just as good, if not more so, and, by far, more fool proof.

SERVE WITH: GRILLED POTATOES À LA MODE DE MA FEMME (p. 34) and *petit pois*. Salad, of course, and a long loaf of French bread.

SPANISH OMELET

2 tbsps. butter
1 onion, cut in large dice
2 green peppers, cut in 1″ chunks
1 1 lb. can tomatoes
½ tsp. salt
¼ tsp. pepper
1 tbsp. corn starch

2 tbsps. water
1 cup cooked green peas
4 2-egg BASIC OMELETS (p. 122) or 2 4-egg BASIC OMELETS

1. Heat the butter in a saucepan. Add the onions and green peppers and sauté them until the onions are golden and the peppers have softened a bit. Add the tomatoes, salt and pepper. Bring the mixture to a boil.

2. Mix the cornstarch and the water. Add this to the tomato mixture. Stir. Reduce the flame. Simmer 30 minutes.

3. Add the cooked green peas. Heat.

PRE-PREPARATION: This sauce may be made in advance and re-heated. Do not, however, add the peas until you re-heat, to avoid overcooking them.

4. Prepare the BASIC OMELETS, one at a time. Fill each with a proportionate amount of the sauce, in the manner prescribed for filling an OMELETTE À LA REINE (p. 122).

CHEDDAR CHEESE OMELET

8 oz. Cheddar cheese, sliced
4 2-egg BASIC OMELETS (p. 122) or 2 4-egg BASIC OMELETS

1. Crumble the Cheddar cheese or use grated cheese, approximately 2 oz. for each two eggs.

2. Prepare the BASIC OMELETS, one at a time, but before each is quite ready to be taken from the pan, cover its entire surface with the prepared cheese. Melt the cheese further by slipping it quickly under a broiler. Then slide the omelet out of the pan, folding it as you would a simple BASIC OMELET.

JELLY OMELET

1 cup red currant jelly
4 2-egg BASIC OMELETS (p. 122) or 2 4-egg BASIC OMELETS

1. Prepare the BASIC OMELETS, one at a time.
2. Fill each omelet with a proportionate amount of the jelly, in the manner prescribed for filling an OMELETTE À LA REINE (p. 122).

The most lush of omelets, which the Cookery cannot afford to offer and yet keep within its very moderate price range, is made exquisitely at home by my wife. It is likely to be beyond your home budget, too, and yet I set it down for the mere enjoyment of its contemplation. I suggest, though, that you pamper yourself with it at least once. There must be something you have done to convince yourself you deserve it. This bit of Utopia is, in common English, a CREAMED LOBSTER OMELET.

CREAMED LOBSTER OMELET

1 recipe MORNAY SAUCE, as for EGGS BENEDICT MORNAY (p. 117)
1 tbsp. butter
2 shallots, chopped (or 2 tbsps. onion, chopped)
2 tbsps. dry white wine

½ tsp. dry mustard
2 tsps. parsley, chopped
2 cups fresh picked lobster meat, cut in large dice
4 2-egg BASIC OMELETS (p. 122) or 2 4-egg BASIC OMELETS

1. Prepare the sauce. Reserve.

2. Melt the butter in a small skillet. Add the shallots and wine and cook until the liquid is reduced by half. Add the mustard and parsley. Add the MORNAY SAUCE. Mix thoroughly.

PRE-PREPARATION: If you want to pre-prepare the filling, stop here. If you were to add the lobster ahead, it would release its liquid into the sauce and render the whole watery and unpleasant.

3. Add the lobster to the sauce mixture and heat.

NOTE: If you have gotten this far, you have a wonderful LOBSTER THERMIDOR. Why in the world you would want to hide it under an omelet is more than I can see. The same goes for the sautéed chicken livers and the creamed chicken, in earlier recipes. Particularly if you cannot produce a really good omelet, unlike the French, just eat the filling and let the omelet go!

4. Prepare the BASIC OMELETS, one at a time. Slide each onto a heat-proof serving dish, filling it with the creamed lobster mixture, in the manner prescribed for filling an OMELETTE À LA REINE (p. 122). Sprinkle the omelets with additional grated Swiss or Parmesan cheese, setting it to melt under a broiler flame.

SERVE WITH: Nothing, as far as we are concerned—it is lush in itself—but neither rice, nor julienne potatoes, nor an elegant green vegetable, will spoil it. Bread is needed.

v. pancaked eggs

The pancaked-egg is not a Cookery innovation—a fact which should surprise no one nor be considered in derogation of eggs pancake style. Their existence and popularity stem from the prairie skillet, the New England farm spider, and the frying pans of neighborhood Jewish delicatessens. In fact, there are some very French *omelettes* that are actually pancaked-eggs, only that the French fold them and so are safe from the inglory of associating themselves with American egg cookery. These eggs are, of course, distinguishable from all others in that what is added to them is cooked in them and becomes one with them. Pancaked-eggs can produce as many variances as you can conjure up fillings—or supply leftovers. They are, therefore, a most useful as well as attractive manner of preparing eggs.

TONGUE AND . . . SALAMI AND . . . CORNED BEEF AND . . . PASTRAMI AND . . . HAM AND . . . BACON AND . . . ETC. AND . . . EGGS, PANCAKE-STYLE

Sauté some variety of meat, fish, or fowl slices lightly in butter, until they are warmed through. Beat eggs—as many as you need—with 1 tbsp. of water per egg. Alter the flame to bright so that the fat becomes quite hot—enough to congeal the eggs quickly when they are added. Add the beaten eggs, keeping the flame high until the underside of the eggs becomes firm, shaking the pan to keep the eggs from sticking. Lower the flame and cook until the pan side of the eggs has browned. Turn and brown the top side—a direction easier given than done. Cookery cooks flip the pancake in mid-air. Do it, if you can; it is the best way. It s a good bit more practical, however, either to use a small pan or to cut the pancake in half before turning, so that a broad spatula can help in the turning. If it breaks, nevertheless, it is simply added proof that life can, at times, be difficult. The resulting mess will have little eye appeal, but it will be as edible as a successfully pancaked-egg.

SERVE WITH: French fries or baked beans, pickles, cole slaw, and/or your favorite condiment.

The all-American WESTERN OMELET *is a form of eggs pancake-style. Instead of its filling, you may add,* à la mode française, *diced, browned potatoes and chopped chives for the classic* OMELETTE PARMENTIER; *cooked, buttered asparagus, sliced, for an* OMELETTE ARGENTEUIL; *small peas for an* OMELETTE AUX PETITS POIS; *sautéed mushrooms for an* OMELETTE AUX CHAMPIGNONS; *smoked Nova Scotia salmon for an* OMELETTE AU LOX*—in fact, it is possible to add almost anything in the refrigerator to the eggs, buy a French dictionary, and get away with it, particularly if your boarders cannot pronounce it. The directions for a* WESTERN OMELET *are a standard guide.*

WESTERN OMELET

8 eggs
8 tbsps. water
3/4 cup ham, diced
3/4 cup onion, chopped
3/4 cup green pepper, chopped
4 tbsps. butter

1. Beat the eggs with the water. Add all the remaining ingredients, except the butter. Mix thoroughly, but lightly.

2. Melt the butter in a skillet. Add the egg mixture and proceed as for EGGS PANCAKE-STYLE (p. 130). Fold as you would a BASIC OMELET (p. 122).

3. If you are wise, to serve 4, you will make four 2-egg omelets, *seriatim,* dividing the filling in equal parts. At most, make two 4-egg omelets, figuring ½ omelet for each of 4 persons. It is all but impossible to make an 8-egg omelet. I would venture an uneducated guess that it has never yet been done, and suggest that you do not try to make omelet history.

vi. odd pans out

CHICKENBURGERS À LA COOKERY

(as distinguished from *à la Mode de ma Femme,* p. 57)

4 cups cooked chicken, finely minced
1 cup canned cream of mushroom soup, undiluted
2 tbsps. grated onion
1 tbsp. lemon juice
salt to taste
2 eggs, beaten with 2 tbsps. water
flour
bread crumbs
shortening for deep frying or butter for shallow frying

1. Combine the chicken with the soup, onion, lemon juice, and salt, mixing thoroughly. Refrigerate until the mixture hardens a bit—about 2 hours. Form the mixture into hamburger-like patties. Try to make at least 8, so that you can serve 2 to a portion. Dip them in the beaten egg, then in flour, and after that in the bread crumbs. Refrigerate again, for at least 1 hour, to permit the coating to congeal.

2. Fry the burgers in deep or shallow shortening, at your option. Either a white or a tomato-based sauce can accompany them, or they can be eaten plain.

SERVE WITH: Grilled tomatoes and any green vegetable. Pick your starch as you please—or skip it.

F-R-I-E-D CHICKEN, SOUTHERN STYLE

1 2½ lb. frying chicken, cut up for frying
1 cup milk
flour
salt and pepper
shortening for deep frying or butter for shallow frying

1. Soak the chicken in the milk for at least 1 hour before cooking time. The milk bath imparts a special delicacy to the flesh inside the later applied coating.

2. Mix the flour with salt and pepper to taste. Dry the chicken and flour it lightly, shaking off the excess flour.

3. Brown the chicken on all sides, in either the deep or shallow fat. From this point forward one's inner convictions as to the true nature of SOUTHERN F-R-I-E-D CHICKEN will govern the final steps of the operation.

PRE-PREPARATION: Believe it or not, these preliminary steps may be done in advance without, in any way, ruining the final product.

4. The Cookery and my husband, who decides the fate of the Cookery's fried chicken, hold with the hard-fried school. His authority for the authenticity of his view, I am sure, is that that is the way his mother made it in Trenton. In any event, to accomplish his end, continue, after browning, to fry the chicken until done, either in deep fat or in the shallow shortening, leaving the skillet open. More simply, transfer the browned chicken to an open pan in a 350 degree oven for about 30 minutes.

5. I hold with the soft-fried school. My authority, un-

questionably, is the way my mother made it in Brooklyn. In addition, it is, in my view, substantially more succulent than the kind my husband likes. After browning the chicken, cover the skillet, turn the light low, and continue to cook it until tender—about 30 minutes.

SERVE WITH: CORN FRITTERS (p. 69) and a Russian-dressed mixed salad; candied or baked sweet potatoes and CREAMY COLE SLAW À LA MODE DE MA FEMME (p. 159). Spaghetti with SPAGHETTI SAUCE À LA MODE DE MA FEMME (p. 34) and a French-dressed green salad, is strictly un-American, but good.

SERVINGS: Most people would say this serves 4. As I have said, I am a firm believer in ½ chicken per person; more so when it is without a rich sauce. From my point of view, this recipe serves 2, with a sandwich left for lunch.

CHICKEN PARMIGIANA

1 recipe of F-R-I-E-D CHICKEN, SOUTHERN STYLE (p. 134)
2 cups of either SPAGHETTI SAUCE À LA MODE DE MA FEMME (p. 34) or, the sauce for LA PIPÉRADE (p. 110)
slices of Mozzarella cheese

1. Prepare the chicken and the sauce of your choice.
2. When the chicken is cooked to doneness, place it in a heat-proof serving platter. Cover each piece with the sauce and a slice of Mozzarella cheese. Slip the platter under the broiler until the cheese melts and browns. This is the Cookery way. I find I get better results by under-cooking the chicken by 15 minutes, dressing it in the man-

ner described, and placing it in a 350 degree oven for 15 to 20 minutes. It seems to me that the cheese melts more evenly and retains a creamier consistency.

PRE-PREPARATION: This dish, if the oven method is used, may be prepared ahead to the point of its being dressed, and then refrigerated. If this is done, permit it ½ hour in the oven to make certain that it is thoroughly hot.

SERVE WITH: A green salad, French-dressed. If a starch seems needed, try either French fried potatoes or POTATO BALLS (p. 54), which can be browned in the oven at the same time the chicken is being finished. Spaghetti, if I may say so, is most inappropriate. If, however, you are of the turn of mind that connects all things Italian with spaghetti, be sure that it is pasta dressed only with butter, to avoid conflict of another sauce with the PARMIGIANA sauce. Better still, bed the chicken in cooked flat noodles or linguine. Your pasta then will profit by the flavor of all that the chicken is heir to.

SAUTÉED CHICKEN LIVERS À LA COOKERY

4 tbsps. butter or oil
2 onions, finely sliced
1½ lbs. chicken livers, halved
salt and pepper to taste
⅛ tsp. sage (optional)
1 tbsp. chopped parsley (optional)

1. Melt the butter or heat the oil in a skillet. Sauté the onions, slowly, until they are almost limp. Raise the flame. Add the chicken livers and sear them on all sides. Add the salt and pepper, lower the flame, and cook the

livers for 8 to 10 minutes. Serve on toast.

2. To change the style to the classic FEGATO VENEZIANA, add the sage and parsley at the time the salt and pepper are added.

3. The manner in which I prefer them to be prepared is as described in OEUFS BROUILLÉS AUX FOIES DE VOLLAILLES (p. 112), except that the livers here are halved instead of sliced.

SERVE WITH: *Petit pois* and French fried potatoes, or over rice or mashed potatoes, accompanied by a salad of your choice—but one that does not include onions.

MIXED GRILL MAISON

½ recipe of SAUTÉED CHICKEN LIVERS À LA COOKERY (p. 136)
4 BEEFBURGERS (p. 57)
12 strips of bacon, grilled

This is not a dish, but a variation on a dish. A little of this and a little of that serves to interrupt the monotony of a lot of one thing. Serve each person a share of the chicken livers on toast, a beefburger, and three strips of bacon. Add to the plate a portion of French fried potatoes or GRILLED POTATOES À LA MODE DE MA FEMME (p. 34) and a broiled tomato half. Dress the plate with watercress. *Et voilà:* a mixed grill of your *maison.*

from the salad board

I NEVER HAD much use for a salad as an end in itself, but I will admit that I am outnumbered and let it go at that. Whatever the cause of your addiction, whether it is the illusion that you may lose weight, or that it is loaded with vitamins, whether you just admire green, or whether you actually like the stuff, the first prerequisite of a decent salad is to get something to complement all that grass. The second is to make it look different from a meadow. The third is to find a substitute for the grass. The fourth is a secret between my wife and myself.* The net result of my prejudices has been that the Cookery salad board works with some of the most expensive ingredients on the menu and turns out platters that are lovely as landscapes—and as edible as it is possible for salads to be.

* To wit: I do not discourage my wife from making salad. I just do not eat it.

i. fish

SALADE NIÇOISE

1 lb. mixed green salad (unless, by chance, you really love the stuff—then suit yourself)
8 oz. tuna fish
4 oz. flat anchovy filets
4 hard-cooked eggs, quartered
4 tomatoes, quartered
1 cup cold cooked string beans (optional)
1 cup cold cooked potatoes, diced (optional)
4 oz. black olives
capers
2 recipes FRENCH DRESSING À LA MODE D'ANNE-MARIE (p. 162), with a clove of crushed garlic added

1. Make a bed of the salad greens in a large salad bowl that can be used for serving. On it arrange the remaining ingredients, other than the dressing, in the most artistic manner possible. It should look like a picture when you are finished.

2. Bring this masterpiece to the table, with the salad dressing in a separate pitcher. Let the diners take a good look at it. After sufficient praise of your handiwork has been offered, pour the salad dressing over all and toss mercilessly. Serve the mixture directly from the bowl.

SERVE WITH: A crusty French loaf. The French employ this salad as a first course in the manner the Californians serve the Caesar Salad. It is also a nice luncheon dish—particularly if you make available a bottle of Rosé or Médoc.

LOBSTER SALAD

4 cups fresh picked lobster meat, diced
2 cups celery, finely minced (not more—it is not celery salad)
1 cup mayonnaise, or to taste, but use a light hand
white pepper to taste (optional)

Mix the ingredients thoroughly and chill.

SERVINGS: Serves 4 to 6, depending on the manner in which it is served.

LOBSTEROLLE

Serve LOBSTER SALAD on a freshly toasted warm hamburger bun or frankfurter roll. Garnish the plate with ripe tomato slices bedded on a leaf of chicory, pickle chips and heated shoestring potatoes.

LOBSTER SALAD SANDWICH

Obviously, put the LOBSTER SALAD between two slices of bread—with lettuce, if you like green.

LOBSTOMATO

Sheer off the top of a ripe tomato, scoop out the pulp and turn it top side down to drain. Fill the hollow to overflowing with LOBSTER SALAD. Underline it with chicory. Mound potato salad and cole slaw on either side—neatly, please, if not artistically.

AVOCADO-LOBSTER SALAD

Use the pit-hole of the avocado as you would the tomato hole in the LOBSTOMATO. Fill it with LOBSTER SALAD. Dress the dish with the usual salad accompaniments or with your own ingenuity.

LOBSTER SALAD WITH RAVIGOTE SAUCE

Mound LOBSTER SALAD on lettuce hearts. Cover it with RAVIGOTE SAUCE (p. 163). Garnish the plate with tomato wedges and quartered hard-cooked eggs. If you really cannot survive a salad without potato salad or cole slaw, by all means, suit yourself.

TUNA FISH SALAD

4 cups canned tuna fish
2 cups celery, chopped
1 tbsp. onion, chopped (optional)
¼ tsp. white pepper (optional)
1 cup mayonnaise or to taste

Drain the tuna fish, flake it and mix it thoroughly with the other ingredients. Chill.

SERVINGS: Serves 4 to 6, depending on the manner in which it is served.

Of course, any form recommended for serving LOBSTER SALAD (p. 143) *will do for* TUNA FISH SALAD*—as long as you recognize that tuna is not lobster. The tuna fish may also be served straight from the can, after draining, dressed with a dressing of your choice and garnished with the trimmings of your choice. In that case, be sure to send along a bit of chopped raw onion or scallion—anything, in fact, to add flavor.*

SALMON SALAD

4 cups canned salmon
1 cup celery, chopped
1 tbsp. scallion, chopped (optional)
¼ tsp. white pepper (optional)
1 cup mayonnaise or to taste

Drain and skin the salmon, flake it and mix it thoroughly with the remaining ingredients. Chill.

SERVINGS: Serves 4 to 6, depending on the manner in which it is served.

SALMON SALAD, *too, may be served in any of the ways prescribed for* LOBSTER SALAD (p. 143). *Like tuna, it may also be used in a steak, untouched, but tastefully dressed and adequately garnished.* CUCUMBER DRESSING (p. 164) *seems to be in favor at the Cookery.*

IMPORTED SARDINE SALAD

Sardines are good only as they come out of the sea, but canned. We are aware of the general preference for the "skinless, boneless," tasteless kind—and serve them. Those *with* skin and bone are, by far, the better. Dress them only with lemon juice. Complete the plate with a type of FRENCH POTATO SALAD (p. 161) and the Cookery's VINEGAR COLE SLAW (p. 159), sliced tomatoes and hard-cooked egg. Since it is a salad, add some green stuff, at least for color.

At home, my wife refuses to waste lobster on a salad, insists tuna fish is for restaurants only and refuses to accept salmon salad as a way of dining. There is a salad time, however, in the life of every cook, including my noble

wife. She will, on rare occasions—like New York dog days, 103 degree fever and, I imagine, earthquake, although I do not know that of my own experience—serve her own superb fish salad, specially garnished, nevertheless, with her profuse apologies. None are needed.

FISH SALAD À LA MODE DE MA FEMME

1 lb. halibut
2 tbsps. scallion, chopped
2 tbsps. India relish, drained
¼ tsp. garlic powder
salt and freshly ground black pepper
½ cup mayonnaise or to taste

1. Dot the halibut with butter, season it with salt, pepper and paprika, and broil it until it is done. Remove the skin and bones. Cool.

2. Flake the fish. Combine it with the remaining ingredients. Refrigerate the salad until serving time.

SERVINGS: Serves 2 to 3—4, only if the garnish is substantial.

ii. fowl

CHILEAN CHICKEN SALAD

½ recipe CHICKEN SALAD (p. 148)
1 cup canned kernel corn
2 tomatoes, seeded and diced

1 large green pepper, diced
½ tsp. salt
¼ tsp. pepper
¼ cup mayonnaise
4 hard-cooked eggs, quartered

1. Prepare the CHICKEN SALAD. Add the remaining ingredients other than the eggs. Mix thoroughly.

2. Set the salad on a bed of lettuce or watercress. Garnish with the hard-cooked eggs.

CHICKEN SALAD

4 cups cooked chicken, diced
¼ cup scallions, finely chopped
½ cup cucumber, diced
salt and freshly ground black pepper
1 cup mayonnaise, or to taste

Mix all of the ingredients and chill.

SERVINGS: Serves 4 to 8, depending on the manner in which you serve it.

CHICKEN SALAD SANDWICHES

CHICKEN SALAD may be served *en sandwich*, plain with a leaf of lettuce, with fine slices of tomato, in combination with crisp bacon—or, in fact, with all three.

CHICKEN SALAD GARNI

CHICKEN SALAD, in combination with potato salad, cole slaw, tomatoes and hard-cooked eggs, enjoys general popularity—although the sameness of the dressings involved is deadly. Try it, instead, with the French dressed VEGETABLE SALAD À LA MODE DE MA FEMME (p. 161) or, for a change, French dress your chicken salad. The over-all difference in palate-appeal will amaze you.

CHICKEN SALAD SURPRISE

Fill a large, scooped-out, drained tomato with CHICKEN SALAD. Serve it on a bed of chicory accompanied, as the Cookery does—and must—by potato salad and cole slaw. Or, vary the monotony, if you will, as has been suggested, by diversifying the dressings on the respective salads—or changing the salad garnishes completely.

CHOPPED CHICKEN LIVER

4 tbsps. shortening, preferably chicken fat
2 large onions, sliced
1 lb. chicken livers, halved
salt and freshly ground black pepper
2 hard-cooked eggs (optional)
4 tbsps. mayonnaise or to taste

1. Melt the shortening in a skillet. In it, sauté the onions until lightly brown. Add the chicken livers and sauté further until the livers are done. [Chicken liver is the most flavorful and best textured liver for chopping. Calves' liver is next best, but not really good. Beef liver is insufferable although, we concede, it is used.]

2. Put the livers and onions (and eggs, if used) through a meat grinder. Mix them with the remaining ingredients, including the pan juices of the skillet in which the livers and onions were cooked. Mix. Chill. It is not advisable to keep chopped liver more than over night and, for flavor, not even that long.

SERVINGS: Serves a minimum of 4. Depending on the manner in which it is served, it can do for as many as 8.

CHOPPED CHICKEN LIVER SANDWICHES

There is only one bread on which to eat a chopped chicken liver sandwich: rye, and one accompaniment: a sour pickle. If you choose to depart from this golden rule, and serve it, for instance, on white toast, note that it will combine well with either bacon or sliced tomato. If you dare, it is dashing with a garnish of raw chopped onion or sliced white radish.

CHOPPED CHICKEN LIVER SALAD PLATTER

Garnish a mound of CHOPPED CHICKEN LIVER with finely chopped hard-cooked egg and raw onion to taste. Surround it with tomato wedges, potato salad and cole slaw, if you wish.

DEVILLED EGGS

6 eggs, hard-cooked
½ tsp. onion, grated, with the juices
½ tsp. Worcestershire sauce
¼ tsp. dry mustard
salt and pepper
mayonnaise

1. Cook the eggs, for no more than 20 minutes, with the water barely at a simmer. Immerse them immediately in cold water. This method of cooking will keep the eggs tender and prevent the yolks from turning green around the edges.

2. Peel the eggs and cut them carefully in half. Remove the yolks and reserve the whites.

3. Sieve the yolks. Add the remaining ingredients to the sieved yolks, with enough mayonnaise to form a creamy mass. Use the yolk mixture to refill the hollows in the egg whites. Chill, but not for too long, or a hard, discolored outer coat will form. Dust with paprika before serving.

SERVINGS: Depend on whether the eggs are used as garnish or as a primary food. In any event, you know how many eggs you can eat.

EGG SALAD

6 hard-cooked eggs
salt and pepper
1 tbsp. mayonnaise per egg, or to taste

Chop the eggs coarsely; combine them with the remaining ingredients. Chill. Many, including myself, like to add to it such things as chopped celery or onion, India relish, or even caviar. My husband—and, therefore, the Cookery—contends that he likes egg salad to taste like egg salad—and let outside influences provide the taste contrasts.

EGG SALAD SANDWICHES

If you like EGG SALAD, it is good with a slice of lettuce between two pieces of bread. It is neutral enough in flavor, however, to accept active condiments. Try it with anchovy strips, a rasher of bacon, slices of tomato, or any combinations or permutations thereof.

EGG SALAD AND ANCHOVY SURPRISE

Fill a hollowed-out, drained tomato with EGG SALAD, mounding it over the top lip of the tomato cup. Criss-cross the mound with anchovy filets. Serve it with FRENCH PO-

TATO SALAD (p. 161)—please!—and VINEGAR COLE SLAW (p. 159) to offset the heavy mayonnaise flavor of the egg salad.

iii. good red herring

Good red herring and its ilk is the most virtuous of all salad fixings: no preparation is required. It comes straight from the neighborhood delicatessen, out of its waxed paper and onto a plate. Nothing could be less taxing than the cold cut platter or, in the end, more appreciated—when the mood for that kind of meal strikes. In fact, the curse is off it: it is not a salad—just good food that is cold.

NOVA SCOTIA SALMON AND CREAM CHEESE PLATTER

It is unwritten scripture that Nova Scotia salmon may not be eaten without cream cheese, and venial sin to eat it on Sunday without bagel. Nonetheless, add to the platter lettuce hearts, tomato wedges, quartered hard-cooked eggs and VINEGAR COLE SLAW (p. 159). No special dispensation is needed.

ASSORTED SMOKED FISH PLATTERS

Use, jointly or severally, sturgeon, smoked white fish, Nova Scotia salmon or lox, kippered salmon, herring filets or whatever else may attract your appetite. Provide lemon quarters, soft cheeses, green pepper rings, radish roses and etceteras. Marinated cold vegetables are a colorful addition, somewhat different, and harmonize well with the fish flavors.

ASSORTED COLD CUT PLATTER

The Cookery assortment is: ham, tongue, turkey and Swiss cheese, garnished with tomato, pickle, potato salad and cole slaw. It might well be to your taste to modify or add: roast beef, veal or lamb, or any of the variety meats in family favor.

ASSORTED CURED MEAT PLATTERS

Singly or in combination, such cured meats as corned beef, pastrami, rolled beef, salami are satisfying with baked beans, cole slaw and, without a doubt, pickles and mustard.

PRINCIPASTO

1 beautiful, large serving platter
1 small head of lettuce, shredded as for cole slaw
1 10 oz. package of frozen mixed vegetables, cooked
1 recipe FRENCH DRESSING À LA MODE D'ANNE-MARIE (p. 162), with a crushed clove of garlic added
4 tomatoes, thinly sliced
8 thin slices of a salami of your choice
10 canned pimentos, halved
8 anchovy filets
4 sardines
black olives
capers

1. Cover the serving platter with the shredded lettuce, concentrating it in a flat, high pile toward the center.

2. Mix the cooked vegetables with the salad dressing. Cover the mounded lettuce with the vegetables.

3. Surround the outside of the mound of lettuce and vegetables with the slices of tomato, standing on end like wagon wheels. Circle the tomatoes with wagon wheels of salami.

4. Cover the outer circle of salami completely with the pimento halves. If 10 are not enough to go around, add more. The appearance should be that of a flower, with the pimentos being the petals and the vegetables the center.

5. Place the remaining ingredients artistically on top of the vegetables. Serve!

SERVE WITH: Chianti! Positively! And Italian bread.

SERVINGS: This is a meal in itself. It is also an attractive way to serve an antipasto to many more than 4 people.

CHEF'S SALAD

I have often wanted to meet the chef who originated this form of salad—in a dark alley. I can think of nothing less suitable for the consumption of carnivores. The base of it is coarsely chopped greens: lettuce, escarole, endive, chicory and the like. Superimposed on this—in fine mockery—are juliennes of ham, turkey and Swiss cheese. It is generally served with a dressing of one's choice. A heavy hand with the meats and cheese, as at the Cookery, will afford some compensation to those upon whom you inflict this creation.

Cottage cheese, like salad meals, is another defect in the American culinary character. It would be only a venial failing if it were taken like medicine but, truth to tell, it is liked. The only mitigating factor is that cottage cheese, like herring, is made by God and the grocer, and requires no expenditure of creative energy on the cook's part.

COTTAGE CHEESE SURPRISE

Scoop the pulp from a tomato and drain it. Fill it with cottage cheese. Set it on a bed of greens. Add portions of potato salad and cole slaw to the platter. Serve a boat of nice salad dressing—at least that.

SPRING VEGETABLES WITH COTTAGE CHEESE AND SOUR CREAM

Dice scallions, radishes and cucumbers in proportions that please you. Place a large scoop of cottage cheese in a soup bowl. Cover it with the diced vegetables and cover them with as much sour cream as you can take. Dust the whole with salt and freshly ground black pepper. Serve it with real black bread.

FRUIT AND COTTAGE CHEESE SALADS

Canned peach halves or pineapple rings—which, fortunately, are always in season—combine well with cottage cheese. So do fresh fruits in their respective seasons. Arrange the fruits and cheese on chicory leaves. The Cookery decorates with scoops of sherbet and even dieters close their eyes to those added calories. A fruity CREAM CHEESE DRESSING (p. 164) may be passed for those who are not dieting or those dieters who never open their eyes while eating.

AVOCADO FILLED WITH FRESH FRUIT SALAD

Fill and over-fill the pit-hole in an avocado with varied fruits of the season, diced. You may be stuck with bananas, grapefruit and oranges in the winter, but Spring and Summer add the color and flavors of melons and berries, as well as the more prosaic but, nonetheless, delicious, peaches, pears and pineapples. Serve with CREAM CHEESE DRESSING (p. 164).

POLYNESIAN MEDLEY

1 small head of lettuce, shredded as for cole slaw
1 3 oz. box of lime jello, prepared in 4 attractive molds
8 oz. fresh or frozen pineapple chunks
4 small bananas
2 oz. shredded coconut
8 preserved kumquats
12 Maraschino cherries

1. On 4 individual serving plates, place a sparse bed of the shredded lettuce. Unmold one portion of jello on each lettuce bed. On one side of the jello, mound approximately 2 oz. of the pineapple chunks.
2. Roll the bananas in the shredded coconut. Place a banana in an advantageous spot on each plate.
3. Garnish each plate attractively with a proportionate share of the kumquats and cherries.

But, between you and us, when it comes to salads, there is nothing like a good schmaltz herring!

iv. garnishes

VINEGAR COLE SLAW

1 medium head green cabbage, shredded and chopped
1 small carrot, finely chopped
1 tbsp. red Spanish onion, chopped
¼ cup vinegar
2 tbsps. sugar
½ tsp. salt
¼ tsp. pepper
¼ tsp. garlic powder

Place the shredded and chopped vegetables in a bowl. Add the remaining ingredients. Mix thoroughly. Refrigerate for at least 2 hours before serving. Mix thoroughly again. Use iceberg lettuce, shredded, instead of cabbage, for a most unusual salad. It is wonderful with POT ROAST OF BEEF À LA MODE DE MA FEMME (p. 68), duck in any form, or any dish that requires a sharp contrast with its flavors.

CREAMY COLE SLAW À LA MODE DE MA FEMME

1 medium head cabbage, shredded
1 small onion, grated
½ cucumber, grated
1 cup sour cream

2 tbsps. sugar
1 tbsp. mayonnaise
1½ tbsps. vinegar
½ tsp. salt
¼ tsp. pepper
1 tbsp. caraway seeds (optional)

Mix all of the ingredients. Chill for at least 2 hours before serving. Mix thoroughly again.

POTATO SALAD

4 cups hot potatoes, diced
6 tbsps. oil
2 tbsps. vinegar
¼ cup onion, finely chopped
2 tbsps. green pickle relish
1 tsp. salt
¼ tsp. pepper
1 cup mayonnaise

1. Boil the potatoes in their jackets. Peel them, while hot, and cut them into large dice. Immediately, pour the oil and vinegar over them and toss lightly to distribute it. This keeps the potatoes from turning black. Set the potatoes aside to cool.

2. Mix the potatoes with the remaining ingredients. Chill.

FRENCH POTATO SALAD

4 cups hot potatoes, diced
4 recipes FRENCH DRESSING À LA MODE D'ANNE-MARIE (p. 162)

Mix all of the ingredients. Refrigerate, but bring to room temperature before serving.

VEGETABLE SALAD À LA MODE DE MA FEMME

1 8 oz. can diced carrots
1 8 oz. can diced beets
1 8 oz. can baby lima beans
1 8 oz. can small peas
½ 8 oz. can kernel corn
½ small onion, finely minced
salt and freshly ground black pepper
¼ tsp. garlic powder
½ cup mayonnaise or to taste—lightly, however, does it

1. Open all of the cans and drain the vegetables thoroughly. Drain the beets separately or the red juices will lend an ugly color to the other vegetables.

2. Combine the vegetables with the other ingredients. Mix thoroughly. Chill. Mix thoroughly again before serving.

3. Instead of mayonnaise, you may use FRENCH DRESSING À LA MODE D'ANNE-MARIE (p. 162) or RUSSIAN DRESSING (p. 163). If you are a macaroni salad fan, add boiled el-

bow macaroni to the vegetable salad mixture for a most unusual kind of macaroni salad. The vegetable components may also be varied to suit your tastes and those of your family, but do not eliminate the beets whether you like them or not. Their color is needed.

v. dressings

FRENCH DRESSING À LA MODE D'ANNE-MARIE

1 tbsp. good wine vinegar
salt and pepper
herbs or spices
2 tbsps. good olive oil

1. Pour the vinegar into the bottom of your salad bowl. Add salt and pepper. Add whatever herbs or spices you choose, *e.g.* garlic, tarragon, chives, basil. Mix, with a spoon, until the seasoning and spices are thoroughly combined with the vinegar. This is absolutely essential—according to Anne-Marie—*before* you add the oil.

2. Add the oil. Mix again until the oil becomes thoroughly integrated with the vinegar mixture.

3. If it is your design to use the dressing for a green or mixed salad, add your salad ingredients, washed and completely free of water, to the dressing—instead of vice

versa—and toss until the leaves are fully coated with the dressing.

On the word of our good friend Anne-Marie, this is the only true French dressing, the Cookery's and other recipes to the contrary notwithstanding. Her salads are always exquisitely dressed. My wife makes her French dressing strictly according to Anne-Marie's recipes. Hers have never tasted as good as Anne-Marie's.

RUSSIAN DRESSING

2 tbsps. mayonnaise
2 tbsps. ketchup or chili sauce
1 tsp. vinegar

Combine the ingredients thoroughly so that no lumps, bumps or clots remain. The proportion of mayonnaise to ketchup or chili sauce may be varied to suit your own taste. Chopped sweet pickle, India relish or prepared horse radish may be added for a change of pace. Once, I mistook the seafood cocktail sauce bottle for the chili sauce and ended up with the best Russian dressing I had ever made.

RAVIGOTE SAUCE

½ cup mayonnaise
½ cup whipped cream
3 tbsps. chili sauce
1 tbsp. lemon juice
½ tsp. salt

1 tbsp. green pepper, finely chopped
1 tbsp. onion, finely chopped
1 hard-cooked egg, finely chopped

Blend all of the ingredients thoroughly and chill.

CUCUMBER DRESSING

½ cup mayonnaise
¼ tsp. dry mustard
½ tbsp. lemon juice
½ tbsp. parsley, chopped
1 cucumber, grated

Mix all of the ingredients thoroughly and chill.

CREAM CHEESE DRESSING

1 4 oz. package cream cheese
sweet cream
2 oz. fruit purée

Add sweet cream to the cream cheese until it is thinned to the consistency of heavy cream. Add a fruit purée of your choice, *i.e.* raspberry, strawberry, or the liquid from Maraschino cherries, adding a few of the cherries, chopped.

supper's on the table

SUPPER IS THE MOST capricious meal of the day. Breakfast, lunch and dinner are eaten to satisfy hunger—supper merely to suppress an itch. Food has been known to appease hunger. Food alone will not propitiate that nameless post-prandial yearning. It takes a certain *je ne sais quoi*. It is the one time of the day that not only permits but demands a departure from the usual.

The Cookery has just that knack with a midnight snack—offered here for your adoption. Not that you ought, by any means, to encourage your family to abandon corn flakes and milk in favor of some gastronomic extravaganza. Let them continue to search the refrigerator and inventory the cupboards—and grumble. But bear in mind, for the time when even you can no longer stand it, our collection of noshes from Neuilly and Nervi—and New York.

i. french toast and french-toasted sandwishes

PAIN PERDU, FRENCH TOAST WITH A FRENCH NAME

1 loaf unsliced white bread
4 eggs beaten with 4 tbsps. milk
shortening for deep frying or butter for shallow frying

1. Cut the bread into single slices the thickness of 3 usual slices of sliced bread. Trim the crusts and cut each slice in half on the diagonal. Three such halves should constitute a portion. Therefore, figure on 6 such slices of bread.

2. Soak the bread slices in the beaten egg until they are well saturated. No arid islands should be discovered upon eating.

3. Drop the soaked bread slices into the deep hot fat and fry them until they are cooked through inside and golden brown on the outside. Drain on absorbent paper. Or, using much butter, hot, fry the toast in a skillet until it is similarly cooked.

4. Sprinkle with powdered sugar for prettiness, if you choose.

SERVE WITH: Bacon or sausage and syrup or jelly.

RÔTIES À L'ORANGE

18 slices white bread, trimmed
orange marmalade

4 eggs beaten with 4 tbsps. milk
shortening for deep frying or butter for shallow frying

1. Make triple-decker sandwiches of the bread and orange marmalade. Cut each sandwich in half the long way. Three halves should be served as a portion.

2. Dip the marmalade sandwiches in the beaten egg, holding the decks tightly together. Saturate them well, as you would French toast.

3. Deep or shallow fry them as prescribed for PAIN PERDU (p. 168). Sprinkle with powdered sugar.

CROQUE MONSIEUR

8 slices white bread, trimmed
4 slices cooked ham
4 slices Swiss cheese
(Swiss Swiss is always better; or Mozzarella cheese—it's cheaper)
4 eggs, beaten with 4 tbsps. milk
shortening for deep frying, or butter for shallow frying

1. Make sandwiches of the bread, ham, and cheese. Moisten the edges of the bread with some of the beaten egg and press them together. Dip each whole sandwich in the remainder of the beaten egg.

2. Fry each sandwich, thus prepared, as prescribed for PAIN PERDU (p. 168).

CROQUE MADAME

8 slices white bread, trimmed
4 slices cooked turkey
4 slices Swiss or Mozzarella cheese
4 eggs, beaten with 4 tbsps. milk
shortening for deep frying, or butter for shallow frying

1. Make 4 sandwiches, each containing 1 slice of turkey and 1 slice of cheese.
2. Prepare and fry them as prescribed for CROQUE MONSIEUR (p. 169).

CROQUE MONTE CRISTO

8 slices white bread, trimmed
4 slices cooked ham
4 slices cooked turkey
4 slices Swiss or Mozzarella cheese
4 eggs, beaten with 4 tbsps. milk
shortening for deep frying or butter for shallow frying

1. Make 4 sandwiches, each containing 1 slice ham, 1 slice turkey, and 1 slice cheese.
2. Prepare and fry them as prescribed for CROQUE MONSIEUR (p. 169).

MOZZARELLA IN CAROZZA

8 slices white bread, trimmed
4 fairly thick slices Mozzarella cheese

4 eggs, beaten with 4 tbsps. milk
shortening for deep frying or butter for shallow frying
16 anchovy filets
capers

1. Make sandwiches of the bread and cheese. Prepare them and fry them as prescribed for CROQUE MONSIEUR (p. 169).

2. Criss-cross the anchovy filets on the finished sandwich tops. Garnish with the capers.

CROQUE CARNEGIE

1 cup cooked tongue, ground
½ cup green pickle relish
2 tbsps. mustard, or to taste
1 tbsp. mayonnaise
8 slices white bread, trimmed
4 eggs, beaten with 4 tbsps. milk
shortening for deep frying, or butter for shallow frying

1. Mix thoroughly the tongue, relish, mustard, and mayonnaise.

2. Sandwich the tongue mixture between each two slices of bread.

3. Prepare the sandwiches and fry them as prescribed for CROQUE MONSIEUR (p. 169).

CHOPPED CHICKEN LIVER MORE-OR-LESS EN CROÛTE

½ recipe CHOPPED CHICKEN LIVER (p. 149)
8 slices white bread, trimmed
4 eggs, beaten with 4 tbsps. milk
shortening for deep frying or butter for shallow frying

1. Prepare the CHOPPED CHICKEN LIVER.

2. Make sandwiches of the bread and liver, thinly spread. Prepare and fry them as prescribed for CROQUE MONSIEUR (p. 169).

Any of the CROQUES *make excellent cocktail tidbits when cut smaller,* i.e., *each sandwich cut in quarters. Special care must be taken, however, that the sandwich quarters are well stuck together before they are fried, or the components will part company in the fat.*

ii. made in france

PISSALADIÈRE

1 recipe of the sauce for LA PIPÉRADE (p. 110)
4 English muffins, split and toasted
grated Parmesan cheese

32 anchovy filets
8 black olives, pitted

1. Prepare the sauce.

2. Spread some of the sauce on each half of English muffin. Cover it heavily with grated cheese. Over the cheese make a square of 4 anchovy filets. In the center of the square, place an olive. Broil until the cheese melts and browns. There is no doubt that the Provençal original does not use English (*Grâce à Dieu!*) muffins. The base is French bread dough, covered with the sauce and the trim, baked in the manner of the better known *pizza.* It would most certainly be praiseworthy were you to be moved to emulate, in full, *les Provençaux.*

To us who have been reared on a deep sepia concoction called onion soup as a first course to a so-called French meal, both what authentic French onion soup looks like and when the French eat it, will come as a surprise. You may, as I do, conclude that the American version is better. You will not, however, be able to disagree with the French that it is the best bet, not before a meal but after a bender —or if you have not been that fortunate, simply as an after-midnight snack with a bottle of good red Burgundy. Either or both are felicitous.

SOUPE À L'OIGNON GRATINÉE

4 large onions, sliced and separated into rings
4 tbsps. butter
1 tbsp. flour
1½ quarts beef consommé
French bread, thinly sliced and toasted
grated Swiss or Gruyère cheese, or, if you must, Parmesan

1. Heat the butter in a large saucepan. Add the onion rings and cook them gently over a low flame until they are golden brown. Sprinkle with the flour and blend well. Raise the flame and gradually add the beef consommé, stirring until the soup comes to a boil. Lower the heat, cover the pan, and simmer gently for 20 minutes. I really hate to say this, but if you are like my husband, or want to short-circuit the preparations, use canned, frozen, or dehydrated onion soup.

2. Place a layer of the toasted French bread slices at the bottom of a deep individual casserole or soup crock and cover them with the grated cheese. Add a portion of the onion soup. Float another layer of the toast slices on top of the soup. Cover them thickly with grated cheese. Put the whole under a broiler flame until the cheese melts and forms a crust.

SERVINGS: **Serves 6.**

iii. pancakes

Those who eat COOKERY BLINTZES believe them to be, without a doubt, the best BLINTZES made. That is not true. They are next best. My mother-in-law's are best. The blintze recipe I offer is my mother-in-law's, not the Cookery's—further evidence, if more is needed, of the fidelity of my public spirit.

BLINTZES BELLEMÈRE

4 eggs, beaten
¾ cup flour
1 cup water
½ lb. cream cheese
½ lb. farmer cheese
2 tbsps. cornstarch
2 tbsps. sugar
1 tsp. vanilla extract
butter for frying

1. Add the flour to 2 of the eggs, incorporating it thoroughly. Add the water, bit by bit, until the batter reaches the consistency of heavy cream. If this consistency is reached before the entire cup of water is used, discard the remainder. If the reverse is true, add additional water until the texture of the batter is correct.

2. Heat a 4-inch skillet. Using a buttered brush, grease the hot pan lightly. Quickly add about 1 tbsp. of

batter, tipping the pan to spread the batter over its entire surface. Cook, briefly, until the batter comes away from the sides of the pan. Turn it onto a fresh towel. Repeat the process until the batter is gone. If your luck holds—none stick—the batter will yield about 20 BLINTZE leaves.

3. Mix the remaining ingredients, including the other 2 eggs, to a smooth paste for the BLINTZE filling.

4. Place 1 to 2 tbsps. of filling on each leaf. Roll, tucking in the edges, into neat packets.

PRE-PREPARATION: The BLINTZES may be made completely and refrigerated until it is time to fry them. Some say they may even be frozen—as they are commercially.

5. Heat butter in a large skillet. In it, sauté the BLINTZES until they are brown on all sides.

SERVE WITH: Sour cream and/or jelly.

SERVINGS: These BLINTZES are smaller than the regulation kind, their texture also being substantially lighter than standard. Twenty of these are equivalent to no more than 8 to 10 of the usual ones, a number easily consumed by 4.

NOTE: The recipes for pancakes which follow are based on one fundamental premise: buy the pancake mix and concoct it according to package directions. This is an honest recognition of a fact of modern life: pancake mixes are *in;* mixing pancakes is *out*. Let your virtue, in lifting pancakes *à l'Américain* out of the rut of sameness, ease your guilt, if any, in your use of this common short-cut to easier living. The end product will not be the worse for it, or I would be more insistent on putting you to work—as well as my wife, who has been unabashed in her use of the mixes—and getting away with it.

BLINI

enough pancake batter, buckwheat, if possible, as per NOTE (p. 176)
12 oz. sour cream
6 oz. red salmon roe caviar

1. Rather than large flapjack-size pancakes, prepare the BLINI in pancakes no more than 3 inches in diameter.

2. Stack the pancakes two to a stack. Serve these stacks 3 to a portion. Top each stack with about 1 oz. of sour cream and, over that, ½ oz. of the caviar.

PRE-PREPARATION: The pancake batter, of course, can be made in advance. The pancakes, as they are being made, can be kept warm in a moderate oven until the total number has been completed.

3. Once the sour cream has been placed on the pancakes, serve them immediately. They will cool quickly because of the cold sour cream. Greater insurance would be to place your caviar-topped sour cream in the center of the plate, circle it with the pancake stacks, and let the guests spoon on their own garnish.

DÉLICE DAUPHINE

enough pancake batter, as per NOTE (p. 176)
12 slices of Canadian bacon, grilled
12 slices, thin, of Mozzarella cheese

1. Prepare the pancakes in the size and number prescribed for BLINI (p. 177). Stack them in two's.

2. Transfer the pancake stacks to an oven-proof serving dish. Top each stack with a slice of the grilled Canadian bacon and a slice of the Mozzarella cheese. Slip the platterful under a broiler flame until the cheese melts and browns a bit.

PANCAKES CUBAINES

⅔ cup canned crushed pineapple, drained
⅓ cup apricot jam
2 tbsps. Rum
enough pancake batter, as per NOTE (p. 176)

1. Mix thoroughly the pineapple, jam, and Rum. Cook for 5 minutes.

2. Prepare the pancakes in the size and number prescribed for BLINI (p. 177). Stack them in two's.

3. Transfer the pancake stacks to an oven-proof serving dish. Top each stack with a proportionate amount of the pineapple mixture. Place the platter under a broiler flame until the topping is glazed.

PANCAKES BAR-LE-DUC

enough pancake batter, as per NOTE (p. 176)
6 oz. red currant jam
powdered sugar

1. Prepare the pancakes in the size and number prescribed for BLINI (p. 177).

2. They are to be stacked in two's. Between each two, sandwich ½ oz. of the jam. Dust the top pancake with powdered sugar.

PANCAKES AU CHOCOLAT

enough pancake batter, as per NOTE (p. 176)
6 oz. grated chocolate
(use sprinkles if you cannot obtain the chocolate)
6 oz. whipped cream
shredded coconut to taste

1. Prepare the pancakes in the size and number prescribed for BLINI (p. 177).

2. They are to be stacked in two's. Between the two, however, distribute about ½ oz. of the grated chocolate. On the top of each stack, plop about ½ oz. of whipped cream, which you decorate with the shredded coconut.

3. Serve quickly enough to prevent the heat of the pancake from melting the whipped cream, or the whipped cream from chilling the pancake.

STRAWBERRY SHORTCAKE PANCAKES

enough pancake batter, as per NOTE (p. 176)
6 oz. fresh or frozen strawberries, sliced (sugar them if

they are fresh)
6 oz. whipped cream

1. Prepare the pancakes in the size and number prescribed for BLINI (p. 177).

2. They are to be stacked in two's. Between each two, place a layer of about ½ oz. of the strawberries. Spread the top pancake in each stack with ½ oz. whipped cream. Garnish with a few slices of the strawberries and a little of the strawberry juice.

iv. spécialités de la maison

NOW YOU CAN DO-IT-YOURSELF

From a platter of assorted salad and sandwich fillings —tuna, egg salad, ham, cheese, salami, tongue, turkey, tomato slices, cole slaw, and pickles, served with rolls, pumpernickel, or breads—create your own palate-pleasing combinations.

SUPPER'S ON THE TABLE

Help yourself from an ample platter of Nova Scotia salmon, smoked white fish, hard-boiled eggs, and cream cheese, garnished with slices of tomato and onion. Served family style.

NOW YOU CAN DO-IT-YOURSELF and SUPPER'S ON THE TABLE, buffet platters served for 2 or 4, are among the most popular selections on the special Cookery supper menus. It all goes to prove, we believe, that cooking does not pay!

index

D

E

R

S

T

U

V

W